NATHAN MADISON

UPROOT

REFRAMING THE FEELING OF
INADEQUACY AND RECLAIMING YOUR
GROUND IN GOD'S KINGDOM

For my wife, Stefanie, whose quiet heart
brilliantly shines the light of Jesus

Blessed is the one who trusts in the Lord, whose confidence is in Him. They will be like a tree planted by the water that sends out its roots by the stream. It does not fear when heat comes; its leaves are always green. It has no worries in a year of drought and never fails to bear fruit.

—Jeremiah 17:7–8

CONTENTS

INTRODUCTION

It's ironic that this book is the first I've published because the feeling of not being good enough is the reason my other writing projects have not yet been completed. In fact, to be completely honest with you, the fear of inadequacy was so present in the inception of this book that I wanted to give up on the idea altogether.

This is someone else's story to tell, I thought.

I don't have it in me.

These doubts entered my mind immediately upon chasing after something I was certain God had called me to. Why is that?

After some reflection, I realized that this doubt in myself had been present for a long time but had gone unnoticed, expressing itself in other unfinished projects and unfulfilled dreams. This simple lie that I wasn't good enough to succeed was so deeply rooted that it had begun to multiply and produce things like isolation and stagnation in my faith.

On a whim in late April of 2019, I decided to watch a webinar on the process of book writing, a webinar that encouraged viewers to write their first book on a topic they would consider themselves experts in. Of course, I had the thought, I'm not an expert in anything. Still, I kept watching.

I was instructed to take out a blank piece of paper, write an idea down in the middle of the page, and—this is the best part—start writing anything and everything that came to mind.

These instructions seemed silly, but because it was a free webinar and I didn't have anything better to do, I played along. What happened next was incredible: the Lord prompted me with a word I could not have seen coming. In a step of faith, at the center of a sheet of loose-leaf paper I wrote the following:

Inadequacy

Feelings, phrases, memories, and ideas related to this word began to flow through my mind faster than I could get them onto the page. Until that moment, I had never realized how deeply I had been affected by the lie that I'm not good enough to fulfill what God had put in my heart.

Over the next few days, it was all I thought about. God revealed to me His plan to use every lie that the enemy had whispered to me over the last six years to demonstrate

His truth to others like me—people with dreams and aspirations that have at some point been ignored, prolonged, or silenced by the same lie.

Like clockwork, the enemy began his advances, too. I had begun to take my role in advancing the kingdom of God seriously, and the enemy was afraid of what I might accomplish. But I saw his attacks coming, ignored his voice, and began outlining the book.

What if I can really do it? I asked myself, imagining the impact in the lives of hundreds, even thousands. Inevitably, the more I was filled with confidence, the louder the doubting voice in my head became: *How could God possibly use me? I've never even published a book before. Not only that, but only a few people have ever read my work. What if I can't explain the concept well enough? What if I've been hyping up a bad idea? Did God really say what I thought He said?*

The process of true growth began when God revealed an important truth to me, which I believe He now wants to reveal to you:

The feeling of inadequacy is your way of knowing that the enemy of God has acknowledged your potential.

Before we dive into all that God wants to show you, please understand: I wrote this book because I have lived with the belief that *I am inadequate* long enough to see it produce a multitude of unhealthy fruits in my life. Each and every word you read left the tips of my fingers with an amount of passion and purpose that I've never felt before. Hours have been spent in careful thought and prayer about the most effective approach to these topics, and I have leaned heavily on the circumstances through which God has delivered me to get here. I may never be a true expert in this field, but my promise is to point you towards the One who is. And my friends, He is faithful.

PART I
THE ROOT SYSTEM

Have you ever seen a fallen tree with a root ball still attached at the base? Think of that root system as the lie that you aren't good enough to succeed in the things God has put in your heart. Prior to being toppled over, that lie was the only thing keeping the tree upright and in a position to produce unhealthy fruit in your life.

Picture this tree in a garden. Imagine that this garden represents your life. It has been designed for a specific purpose—a purpose that must be nurtured and protected from harm. Our God desires for us to flourish within His kingdom, for the advancement of His kingdom, but the enemy's lies cause our "purpose in life" to bring about feelings of confusion and uncertainty just as easily as joy and excitement.

As you read this book, I want you to begin considering the areas of your life that could be seen as weeds in a garden—things that draw attention away from the garden's intended purpose. Everything you read leading up to the concluding chapters will be centered around this comparison, beginning with Part I: The Root System.

Together, we are going to acknowledge and take up our swords against the enemy because the truth is this: God has chosen us to advance His purpose for the world and it's our responsibility as the body of Christ to *uproot* the lies that suppress the greatness instilled in each of us.

1

A DROP IN THE BUCKET

When faced with any issue, no matter the size, our first question should be, "What has God said about this?" The Bible is the inspired Word of God. It is a compilation of human thoughts with divinely appointed meaning and value. We read the Bible to know God in a personal way, to recognize that He is everything we need, and to remember that He has already spoken on the things we will encounter in life.

Studying the Word of God allows us to connect and empathize with those throughout history who have struggled with temptation and trials of all kinds. The stories of these men and women are meant to help in our pursuit of freedom and the kingdom of God.

When I began writing this book, I realized that some of the Bible stories I had heard a hundred times are centered around the feeling of inadequacy. We're going to take a look at three such stories, which, throughout the course of this book, we will reference regularly. The first is one that I'm certain you have heard before, and it's centered around the disciple Philip, five loaves of bread, and two fish.

To set the stage for this story, Jesus and his disciples had just crossed the Sea of Galilee and were followed by a substantial crowd. The masses of people were inspired to follow them after witnessing Jesus performing miracles in other towns. Many were so amazed and invigorated that they simply left their homes and occupations without any immediate plans of how long they would be gone or how they would sustain themselves. Standing before Jesus and the wonders He had performed in the lives of the sick and dying reinvigorated them; in those moments, there was nothing more important than following the Messiah.

But what occurred between the extraordinary and the ordinary? What did the people do when their eyes were once again fixed on ordinary human struggles like exhaustion and hunger?

They grumbled.

Now, I imagine a collective sea of discomfort didn't break out all at once, but perhaps the discomfort happened as a result of a gradual groan that began with a few. The few could have been doubters who had only come along to disprove that Jesus was performing miracles as the rumors suggested. That's speculation, of course, but it's common for those half-invested to be the first to complain when conditions become difficult or unpredictable.

Complaining is infectious and can swiftly influence everyone, even those faithfully invested from the beginning.

Regardless of how the tides changed, Jesus perceived that there were people in the crowd who would be returning to their homes after a physically, mentally, and emotionally exhausting series of events. He was filled with compassion for each one of them, perhaps knowing that many would collapse from fatigue in their travels home. So He took action, and that action was engaging a particular disciple whose faith was, evidently, underdeveloped in comparison to some of the others:

> When Jesus looked out and saw that a large crowd had arrived, he said to Philip, "Where can we buy bread to feed these people?" He said this to stretch Philip's faith. He already knew what he was going to do. Philip answered, "Two hundred silver pieces wouldn't be enough to buy bread for each person to get a piece." (John 6:5–7 MSG)

The first thing to notice here is this: Jesus already had a plan. He knew exactly what He wanted to do but intentionally chose to involve Philip when He did. You see, Jesus never acted out of self-interest. One of His primary concerns was to develop those around Him by stretching their faith and pushing them closer to the Father. Not only was He able to see the "big picture" issue, but He was also paying exceptional personal attention to one man whose body was in the right place, but whose heart needed to be pushed to greater limits. Jesus saw the problem and created a solution that would meet the physical needs of the masses and address Philip's propensity to focus on the feeling of inadequacy when faced with something out of his comfort zone.

There is nothing we can do to help these people, was Philip's fear. *The obstacle before us is too great.*

Isn't the disciple's reaction relatable? You and I could surely talk for hours about all the times we have had similar thoughts. Why is it that faith can be so second nature? How did we go from walking with God in the Garden of Eden to such doubt? Often, the first step we need to take is small but hidden by walls of disbelief. Luckily for us, Jesus sees both our difficulties and our resolutions; we must only make it a habit to lean in, listen, and take action.

In the case of Philip, Jesus planned to demonstrate this process through a young boy with an inadequate amount of food, but the right amount of faith:

> One of the disciples—it was Andrew, brother to Simon Peter—said, "There's a little boy here who has five barley loaves and two fish. But that's a drop in the bucket for a crowd like this." (John 6:8–9 MSG)

Like Philip, Andrew was too focused on what they were lacking. They did not yet understand that Jesus was embodying one of the ways in which God develops His people: He commands us to act while allowing us room to doubt. This position of trust is uncomfortable, but faith is about denying self-imposed comfort zones and recognizing that God can and will do what He says He will do. He does not start things that He does not plan to finish. His faithfulness is perfect. And so we read:

> Jesus said, "Make the people sit down." There was a nice carpet of green grass in this place. They sat down, about five thousand of them. Then Jesus took the bread and, having given thanks, gave it to those who were seated. He did the same with the fish. All ate as much as they wanted. When the people had eaten their fill, he said to his disciples, "Gather the leftovers so nothing is wasted." They went to work and filled twelve large baskets with leftovers from the five barley loaves. (John 6:10–13 MSG)

Have you ever felt like Philip and Andrew? Like God has called you to do something but has not properly equipped you? Take comfort in knowing that this is probably by design and that He is trying to stretch your faith. The following are circumstances you may find yourself in from time to time:

- God has not called me to anything because I lack a certain skill set.

- God has called me, but I'm not quite ready yet. I need to grow spiritually before I'm good enough to take action.

- I allowed the truth that God's timeline is different than man's to become a crutch; it became an excuse to do other things I know God has not called me to.

I want you to know that God does not intend to confuse us. When we consider the things He has called us to, we must defend ourselves from feelings of doubt and uncertainty by comparing them with what He has already promised. And what He has promised is to work all things for the good of those who love Him and are called according to His purpose (Romans 8:28).

The word "work" in this verse implies that there is a concentrated effort involved with molding and shaping our circumstances. "All things" reminds us that there are no conditions for God's faithfulness with regard to those He has called. Our Father will always devise a future that frustrates the devil's sense of victory; with every circumstance, good or bad, He creates a future opportunity for there to be a positive impact on the kingdom.

But it tends to take time for us to see that reality, doesn't it? For me, it was six years before I recognized how negatively the enemy had influenced my impact and how quickly God could turn things around for His Glory.

It doesn't have to be that long for you. Whatever has happened in your life, whether it was a mistake you made, a result of stagnancy in your faith, or something that another person did to you, be reminded today that our God can use what has happened for good. The process has not been what you thought it would be like, perhaps, but I promise you, if you keep fighting and pressing into Him, the finished product will be beautiful and filled with purpose.

And the best part? You don't have to have all the answers to move forward.

That is what Jesus was trying to demonstrate to Philip and Andrew. God takes those who don't have it all together to accomplish incredible things for His kingdom and His Glory. Philip's faith was inadequate, but Christ saw greatness and gave him the opportunity to grow. He wanted to show the disciple the possibility of moving from fact and logic into trust and security. And how better to practice trust than to put it into action?

Jesus then challenged the disciples to do something illogical: move from their comfort zone and into the crowd to have everyone sit down to be fed. Can you imagine the thoughts going through their heads? It was no longer about their own skepticism; they now had to look thousands of hungry men, women, and children in the eyes while trusting that Jesus was able to do what He said He could do.

Of course, they were right to trust Him, because every person across that field of green ate more than their fill of bread and fish. Not only that, but there were twelve baskets of leftovers! Jesus demonstrated the faithfulness of God and also that it is not in God's nature to begin something without finishing it.

Jesus wanted Philip to learn to react to future situations from a place of faith, being aware that Jesus would never ask him to do something impossible. Sure, it would have been impossible for Philip alone, but with God Philip could act. To the disciples themselves it seemed like they had inadequate resources, but did they really? It seemed that they were not equipped to succeed, but weren't they? In the end, the true resource was God's blessing.

It was never about the number of biscuits or fish they had, but how those few could be multiplied through faith.

This story, like the other two we will look at in the coming chapters, is proof of God's workmanship. It is evidence of a Father who cares deeply about the development of His children and who takes pride in the process He has laid out, which is built upon faith. But know this: the enemy has a process too, which we will delve into a bit later. His schemes are abundant, and his plan is to steal, kill, and destroy the fullness of life which Jesus came to offer us (John 10:10). When Jesus stretched Philip's faith, I want you to see that he also prevented the enemy's kingdom from advancing. You see, it is fundamentally important that we recognize that the enemy, too, has a plan for our lives. Like God, he plants seeds and cultivates them; he invests in his kingdom with the goal of making it a bigger place.

Acknowledging this truth, consider what might have happened if steps of faith had not been taken in every biblical story you have ever encountered. What if Moses had believed the lie that he was not good enough to deliver the Israelites from captivity? What might have happened had Jesus allowed Philip's doubt to dictate the story of the five thousand? We can't really know what would have transpired, but we can be certain that thousands would not have witnessed the great faithfulness of God that day, or His favor on the man who claimed to be His Son. By the enemy's record, that would have been a great victory.

What I believe God wants us to consider is this: if we are not actively advancing the kingdom of God, are we passively advancing the kingdom of our enemy? Take note of this question, as we will revisit it several times throughout this book.

Before moving on, take some time to acknowledge the ways in which the enemy has attempted to keep you from God's plan for your life. Consider the following questions:

- What has God inspired me to do, and how has the enemy tried to slow my journey?

- What skills has God given me that Satan might view as a threat?

- How might the enemy try to prevent me from hearing God's voice?
- What is present in my life that could be keeping me from being the best version of myself?

2

WHO AM I?

Considering the "giants" of the Christian faith, there are few who had as profound an impact as Moses. This was a man who delivered a burdened and oppressed people from captivity and into a land of their own, and a man who received a divine revelation from God through which a new foundation of moral law was accepted. But before all of these things, Moses lived with some of the things many of us struggle with: inaction, anger, sin, and doubt.

If you are unfamiliar with the story of Moses, it takes place after Joseph and his generation passed. A new Pharaoh came into power in Egypt who had no respect for Joseph's good reputation and no desire to uphold the favor of the Israelites. When Pharaoh noticed that the Israelites (also known as the Hebrews) had become numerous, he drove them into harsh slave labor and commanded the Hebrew midwives to kill any male child born to a Hebrew woman. Pharaoh did this in fear that his authority would be challenged if the Hebrews grew to the point of outnumbering the Egyptians. Another fear may have been that the descendants of Israel would join forces with one of Egypt's many enemies to create an army that Pharaoh could not overcome. Without Joseph or his brothers to contest the decision, the Hebrew people were forced into a long period of darkness and obscurity.

These were the conditions under which Moses was born. Every human right had been stripped from the Hebrew people along with God's command for them to be fruitful and multiply the earth. Every newborn Hebrew boy was cast into the Nile River, never to know life or the God who formed him in his mother's womb. This was to be the fate of Moses, too, but God spared him. In fact, the place he was meant to die was the very place he found life. Through a series of events that could have only been divinely appointed, Moses was found floating on the Nile and was adopted by Pharaoh's daughter to be raised as an Egyptian.

Moses spent his childhood and adolescence in an atmosphere of extravagance and indulgence while his own people were oppressed and mistreated. As he became a man, he began to see the truth, and this awakened a hatred for the mistreatment of his people:

> One day, after Moses had grown up, he went out to where his own people were and watched them at their hard labor. He saw an Egyptian beating a Hebrew, one of his own people. Looking this way and that and seeing no one, he killed the Egyptian and hid him in the sand.

The next day he went out and saw two Hebrews fighting. He asked the one in the wrong, "Why are you hitting your fellow Hebrew?" The man said, "Who made you ruler and judge over us? Are you thinking of killing me as you killed the Egyptian?" Then Moses was afraid and thought, "What I did must have become known." When Pharaoh heard of this, he tried to kill Moses, but Moses fled ... (Exodus 2:11–15)

So where did Moses find himself? Physically, he went to the region of Midian. But spiritually, mentally, and emotionally? He was empty. Being apart from everything he had ever known and loved, Moses was defeated. For perhaps the first time in his life, there was a problem before him that could not be solved with the wealth and influence of his adopted family. He was now an orphan and a fugitive.

Was this what God intended for the life of Moses? Was it God's plan for him to become a murderer? Of course not. Moses had been in a unique position as the adopted son of Pharaoh and could have tried, over time, to leverage that relationship to encourage Pharaoh to loosen his grip on the Israelites. Instead, he acted in a way that resulted in the death of an Egyptian man who may have had a wife and children who he never returned to.

I don't mean to say that Moses was wrong to intervene on behalf of the Hebrew whom the Egyptian was abusing. He certainly should have done something to put a stop to the mistreatment, but his approach was not effective.

Taking the conflict to the source of the issue, Pharaoh, would have been a better approach, and this was ultimately what God would have Moses do in this story of redemption.

Pause for a moment and consider if you, like Moses, have ever allowed anger or bitterness to take root in your life. Have you fled from conflict or held on to the shame of a past mistake? If so, be reminded through the story of Moses that God is passionately redemptive.

After having fled from Egypt, Moses settled down with a woman named Zipporah and had a child. Many years passed and Pharaoh eventually died, and God decided that it was time to establish Moses as a leader and initiate what would become the Hebrew people's exodus from Egypt:

> Now Moses was tending the flock of Jethro his father-in-law, the priest of Midian, and he led the flock to the far side of the wilderness and came to Horeb, the mountain of God. There the angel of the Lord appeared to him in flames of fire from within a bush. Moses saw that though the bush was on fire it did not burn up. So Moses thought, "I will go over and see this strange sight—why the bush does not burn up." When the Lord saw that he had gone over to look, God called to him from within the bush, "Moses! Moses!" And Moses said, "Here I am." (Exodus 3:1–4)

Isn't it interesting that God revealed Himself to Moses through a burning bush when He could have done it in so many other ways? God always acts with purpose and meaning, so what can we suppose was the reason for this revelation? Perhaps God wanted to awaken Moses' past with something restless, painful, and unceasing. Many years had passed since Moses fled from Egypt, so perhaps he needed to be reminded of an ongoing battle that he was meant to fight. In fact, it was a war he had abandoned, and the flames were still burning as strong as ever.

So what did Moses do next? He was immediately filled with zeal for his people, confidence in his abilities, and courage to succeed, right? Not at all. He actually did something that many of us tend to do when considering the things God has called us to. He doubted God's wisdom:

> The Lord said, "I have indeed seen the misery of my people in Egypt. I have heard them crying out because of their slave drivers, and I am concerned about their suffering. So I have come down to rescue them from the hand of the Egyptians and to bring them up out of that land into a good and spacious land, a land flowing with milk and honey—the home of the Canaanites, Hittites, Amorites, Perizzites, Hivites, and Jebusites. And now the cry of the Israelites has reached me, and I have seen the way the Egyptians are oppressing them. So now, go. I am sending you to Pharaoh to bring my people the Israelites out of Egypt." But Moses said to God, "Who am I that I should go to Pharaoh and bring the Israelites out of Egypt?" (Exodus 3:7–11)

The words "Who am I?" echo in my head every time I read those verses. I know the self-deprecating question all too well, and perhaps you do too. It's the question of someone who allows their identity to be determined by their weaknesses; it's the uncertainty of someone who believes that God requires perfection. But nothing could be further from the truth. You don't have to be perfect to pursue the kingdom of God or your purpose. In fact, He will often give us glimpses into the future of the things He has called us to as a way to demonstrate His faithfulness and spur us onward. He gives these assurances not because He has to, but because a Father loves to encourage His children:

> And God said, "I will be with you. And this will be the sign to you that it is I who have sent you: When you have brought the people out of Egypt, you will worship God on this mountain." (Exodus 3:12)

God gave Moses something to look forward to. It was an assurance that the Hebrew nation would one day worship the God of Israel as free men and women outside of Egypt's oppression. Do you know what He didn't do? He didn't tell Moses that it would be easy. But He hinted at faith being critical, and faith ultimately brought success to the journey.

God pursued Moses the way He pursues me and you. You see, this book may find its way into the hands of a person across the world, and I'll never know if it helped until I meet my Father in Heaven and hear the story. In the same way, I'll never hear that story if I sit on my hands and continue believing that I'm not good enough to complete the book as He has called me to.

The same is true for you. There is a unique place for you in the kingdom of God whether or not you know exactly what that looks like right now. Truthfully, you may never know all that you are meant to accomplish with your life, but if you seek the heart of God in every season, He will lead you through your purpose and tell you all the hidden details in Heaven.

Your ability to succeed in the dream God has given you (or has yet to give you) has everything to do with who God is and what He says about you. The fact that He has given you life is a declaration that you are enough. Like Moses, we must make a conscious effort to step away from the lie of inadequacy and towards the truth found in expectancy. We must face our enemy and watch as God breathes life into everything we do, multiplying our efforts as only He can.

But we can't stop there. God showed Philip and Moses what He was able to accomplish if they stepped out in faith, but what about doubt in the midst of trials? The next and final story concerns a man who had no trouble stepping out, but doubted God along the way. Before diving into Peter's story, reflect on the following questions:

- Has a sin or unhealthy environment created a stronghold between myself and God?

- Would I hold on to my past and suppress the voice of God, or would I approach the burning bush?

- Do I dive in faithfully but doubt along the way? Do I make excuses not to begin at all?

- Which voice has been louder in my life, doubt or assurance?

3

AGAINST THE WAVES

Your spirit longs to be used effectively in the advancement of God's kingdom. To remove all that hinders you from chasing after Him is what God desires for you, and so He asks that you listen when He prompts you. And not just when He calls you to a dream, but during the process of fulfilling that dream.

The lie of inadequacy and the byproducts that accompany it are not from God. They are schemes of our enemy who watches and waits for the right moment to spin his webs. Unlike God, the enemy's desire is to keep us within a cycle of doubt and unrest, and the easiest way he accomplishes this is by causing us to lose sight of Jesus.

Faith, as we have seen in the stories of Philip and Moses, is about being shown a problem and having the strength to take a single step forward. Faith is about having the courage to move into uncertainty. But it is not only about the first step, is it? Through the life of Peter, we see that faith is just as much about each step that follows.

This story takes place right after Jesus fed the five thousand, the story we looked at in chapter 1. Christ had the disciples set out on the Sea of Galilee while He went up onto a nearby mountainside to pray and commune with the Father. While Jesus was away, a great storm stirred up and moved across the sea to where the men were located:

> Immediately Jesus made the disciples get into the boat and go on ahead of him to the other side, while he dismissed the crowd. After he had dismissed them, he went up on a mountainside by himself to pray. Later that night, he was there alone, and the boat was already a considerable distance from land, buffeted by the waves because the wind was against it. Shortly before dawn, Jesus went out to them, walking on the lake. When the disciples saw him walking on the lake, they were terrified. "It's a ghost," they said and cried out in fear. But Jesus immediately said to them: "Take courage! It is I. Don't be afraid." (Matthew 14:22–27)

The enemy sought to use the storm to his advantage in a time when the disciples were growing quickly in their faith. Friends, this is what he does. Out of fear, the devil makes advances while God is propelling us forward. Remember, when the enemy tempts you to believe that you are not good enough, that is your way of knowing he sees your potential. Let that truth fill you with motivation to be a champion for your calling in life. Jesus desires this for you in the same way He wanted it for the men He chose to be His disciples. As they traveled together, Jesus was leading them on a journey that could be equated to a life-sized trust fall. These were men who had left everything they knew to live an uncertain and questionably crazy life with someone who claimed to be the Son of God. This journey would either cause them to be cast out from society, or it would be the most meaningful thing they had ever been a part of. Jesus knew, of course, that it would be the latter.

> "Lord, if it's you," Peter replied, "tell me to come to you on the water." "Come," he said." (Matthew 14:28–29a)

Not to take away from the courage of Peter, but isn't it strange that Philip was not the one to have spoken up? Jesus had just fed the five thousand earlier that day, yet Philip didn't make a sound when Jesus revealed Himself in the middle of the storm. How is it that they had just spent so much time in closeness, yet the disciple did not recognize Him? This is a small detail, but so relatable. What we see between the lines of the text reminds us that the men and women of the Bible were real people with struggles that you and I face today.

Whether the Scriptures specifically mention it or not, we can safely assume that several of the disciples on that tossing ship lost sight of who was meant to anchor them in the storms of life. If Jesus healed the sick and dying and gave the blind sight, couldn't He protect them from wind and rain? For Philip, his silence may have been caused by the fear of drowning, or perhaps it was because he realized just how far they were from land and comfort. Maybe he was thinking of the family and security he had left behind to walk with Jesus, and for what? To drown in the open ocean?

As we study this storm, it's important to recognize the similarities between the thoughts of the disciples and our own thoughts today. Have you ever felt that you were far from comfort while in pursuit of the kingdom of God? Have you ever felt that everywhere you turned something was against you? If there is one thing I've learned since giving my life to Christ, it's that the enemy of God will stop at nothing to see me fail.

When you recognize the importance of advancing the kingdom of God and start moving forward, Satan responds by using the storms of life to create doubt and insecurity.

Our enemy will tempt you with lies to cause stagnancy in your faith and to make you distracted and hopeless. These are two examples of the unhealthy fruits we will look at later in the book, but for now, know this: the lie that you are not good enough does not exist on its own. It spreads like kudzu into other areas of your life, often in so many different directions that it becomes difficult to trace back to the source. That's why we, like Peter, desperately need Jesus.

Faith is strengthened through doubt and seasons of obscurity. It is fortified through storms and through taking steps out of what seems like safety and into what is chaotic and uncertain. But it's also about maintaining focus.

Jesus responds promptly to Peter's test by saying, "Come." As followers of Christ, we have to be careful about putting Jesus to the test because He'll take us up on it. There is a dark and hurting world all around us, and there is no shortage of those filled with instability, hopelessness, uncertainty, confusion, and feelings of worthlessness and shame. These people are in grocery stores, your dentist's office, and potentially your own home.

Don't wake up in the morning intending to meet Jesus in the water if you aren't expecting Him to lead you. Because He will. He'll stretch your faith so quickly that you will find yourself wondering how you ever doubted His ability to use you in the first place.

This feeling of fulfillment is found in circumstances of great significance, like leading someone to know Christ as their Savior, but it's also found in the little things, like tipping an extra ten dollars or paying for the car behind you in a fast food drive-through and leaving a note behind that says something simple, like "God loves you." There are so many ways in which Jesus will lead you to be a light in this dark world. All you have to do is keep your heart open to the truth that your impact on this world begins with being the person God made you to be. And only that person.

The truth is, we each have strengths and weaknesses, like Peter, which allow us to connect with people all around us. Your approach to an uncertain situation may look completely different than your neighbor's. The disciples that remained in the boat might have been stronger than Peter in other areas, but they learned from him that day as they watched him walk towards Jesus on the water. Even though it wasn't perfect, even though he doubted Jesus along the way, at least he had the courage to step out:

> Then Peter got down out of the boat, walked on the water and came toward Jesus. But when he saw the wind, he was afraid and, beginning to sink, cried out, "Lord, save me!" Immediately Jesus reached out his hand and caught him. "You of little faith," he said, "why did you doubt?" (Matthew 14:29b–31)

Ultimately, overcoming uncertainty isn't just about you. It's about pointing other people towards Christ. This should be our objective in everything we do. We don't pursue righteousness or step out in faith to boast about doing so (Matthew 6:1), but rather so we can then step out of the way and allow others to see that it was God behind it all. When things get tough, when you doubt God during storms and lose sight of Jesus, never forget how many people you will help by pushing through and pointing to the reason why you made it.

> And when they climbed into the boat, the wind died down. Then those in the boat worshiped him, saying, 'Truly, you are the Son of God." (Matthew 14:32–33)

Faith does not need logic. In fact, logic is perhaps the greatest enemy to faith and is the very reason Christ encourages us to be childlike (Matthew 18:3). By the end of this book, my prayer is that you will see the greater picture of the enemy's schemes and know in your heart that any feeling of inadequacy you're experiencing is about so much more than you. We serve a God who has no limits, and He is pleading with you to put your foot down and work alongside Him to *uproot* the lie that says you aren't good enough.

The battle against your God-given calling is a real one, and the enemy of God fears what might happen if your talents are put to the right use. Satan and his legions watch closely and shudder at the thought of you reaching your full potential. Feeling threatened is the very thing that makes our enemy work as hard as he does to generate negativity and pain in your life. Remember, he has come to steal, kill, and destroy the very life that Jesus came to spread freely (John 10:10).

But the truth is this: Satan's schemes are not new. Just as God is the same today, yesterday, and forever (Hebrews 13:8), the same can be said of our enemy. In the next chapter, we're going to take a closer look at who the enemy is, because you can't win a war if you don't understand exactly who you're fighting and what their stake in the battle is.

Before moving on, take a moment to reflect on the following questions:

- What is my storm in this season?
- What has God delivered me from?
- Do I have a faith-filled person in my life who doesn't just "talk the talk"?
- In what ways can God use me to brighten someone's day, even if just a little?

4

THE LESSER KING

Spiritual warfare is inevitable in this life. That is something we have to come to terms with as followers of Christ. The enemy of God was present in the lives of Philip, Moses, and Peter, sowing seeds of doubt and uncertainty to keep them from moving towards the call of God. He is present in your life as well, doing the same thing. Earth is a battle-field and there is a war going on at all times whether we choose to acknowledge it or not.

A river runs whether or not you're there to see it. In the same way, the enemy of God continues scheming whether or not we're paying attention to him. Wars are not won by pretending the enemy isn't there. They are won by acknowledging the presence of the enemy and then spend-ing intentional time learning his motives, habits, and limitations. This will help us to be armed and prepared for battle and will bring us continuous victory. Because, the truth is, self-doubt and the feeling of inadequacy will come back time and time again in your life; this book is meant to show you how it can be recognized and warred against, but the enemy is not going anywhere between now and when Jesus returns.

So who is God's enemy? Most commonly, he is known as Satan, Lucifer, and the father of lies. God described him in the following way through the prophet, Ezekiel:

> You were the seal of perfection, full of wisdom and perfect in beauty. You were in Eden, the garden of God; every precious stone adorned you: carnelian, chrysolite, and emerald, topaz, onyx and jasper, lapis lazuli, turquoise, and beryl. Your settings and mountings were made of gold; on the day you were created they were prepared. You were anointed as a guardian cherub, or so I ordained you. You were on the holy mount of God; you walked among the fiery stones. (Ezekiel 28:12–14)

God speaks of Satan as if he was something to be proud of at one time; however, the modern-day perception and caricaturization of Satan paints a different picture. Movies and television imagine him to be a red-skinned man with pointed teeth, horns, and a pitchfork, which could not be further from the truth. This may seem like an obvious thing to point out, but it's important that we acknowledge the true image of our enemy to better understand how he operates.

He is not a red-skinned devil, but a being of such mastery that God described him as the "seal of perfection, full of wisdom and perfect in beauty." The way Satan is depicted in the entertainment industry is harmful because it implies that Satan is vile and detestable by nature, which is not true. Before being cast from Heaven, Satan was one of the most precious of God's creations and was one of the closest beings in proximity to God's throne at all times. As a guardian cherub, he stood next to God until he began to admire the throne and believe himself worthy of it.

> You were blameless in your ways from the day you were created till wickedness was found in you. Through your widespread trade, you were filled with violence, and you sinned. So I drove you in disgrace from the mount of God, and I expelled you, guardian cherub, from among the fiery stones. Your heart became proud on account of your beauty, and you corrupted your wisdom because of your splendor. (Ezekiel 28:15–17a)

He was so beautiful and convincing that one-third of Heaven's angels followed him (Rev. 12:4). They believed then, and still believe to this day, that Satan is entitled to the throne of God. The prophet Isaiah refers to our enemy this way:

> How you have fallen from heaven, morning star, son of the dawn! You have been cast down to the earth, you who once laid low the nations! You said in your heart, "I will ascend to the heavens; I will raise my throne above the stars of God; I will sit enthroned on the mount of assembly, on the utmost heights of Mount Zaphon. I will ascend above the tops of the clouds; I

will make myself like the Most High." But you are brought down to the realm of the dead, to the depths of the pit. (Isaiah 14:12–15)

It's important to understand the image of our enemy because the way he looks allows us to better understand how he behaves and how we are affected by his schemes. In reality, Satan is just as commanding and convincing as William Wallace in Mel Gibson's *Braveheart*. He is not ugly or repulsive, but would be one of the most handsome and charismatic of God's creations who has ever existed.

This is echoed in the way he tempts us with things that seem desirable, like sex, money, and fame, which he claims will satisfy us. Many of the lies he tells don't appear to be lies, which is why we call him a wolf in sheep's clothing. He sneakily multiplies our desires and creates envy and pride, but ultimately leads us into failure and sadness, and often depression, when we do not live up to our own expectations.

Earth is Satan's kingdom (John 12:31). Although man was given dominion over the earth, Satan has a motive, an agenda, and the ability to influence our actions. Which begs the question—why did God create man to live in a place where Satan would reign? Such a place was necessary for God to receive the kind of love He desired: a love given by free will and in light of other things that provide pleasure and enjoyment.

Free will is your ability to choose; it is the capability of human beings to comprehend the results of our actions and choose the ones which bring the desired result. Whether that fulfillment is momentary or lasting, right or wrong, left or right, is irrelevant. What matters is that we are able to choose.

Free will is having a mind that is able to roam wherever it wants to roam and a body to take it wherever it wants to go. The innermost desire of our God, in creating us, was that our will would lead us to Him in every circumstance. He wants us to know and trust that He is the only thing truly worthy of our love and affection.

In Genesis, God commands Adam and Eve to be fruitful and to rule over the fish in the sea and the birds in the sky, over the livestock and all the wild animals, and over all the creatures that move along the ground (Genesis 1:26). The simple fact that God had to command them to act a certain way shows us that there was no coercion involved with living out the will of God. By God having said to Adam and Eve that they could eat from every tree in the garden except for the one in the middle (Genesis 3:3), referring to the tree of the knowledge of good and evil, we can see that He gave them *guidelines*, but intentionally allowed them the freedom to choose their own path.

King David pleaded with God to make his heart clean and to renew a steadfast spirit within him (Psalm 51:10). The implication here is that man's heart can become wayward on its own, and we can all find ourselves far from Him by our acts of free will. Jesus reminded His followers that the mouth relays the things that fill the heart (Luke 6:45), and Paul reminded the Corinthians of a long list of sins that we should be fighting each day (1 Corinthians 6:9–10).

These sins are Satan's craftsmanship. You and I have the ability to choose, of course, but the original sin in the Garden of Eden took place as the result of the enemy's persuasion, and every sin that has thus followed is impacted by his desire for us to suffer.

It's important to remember what we know about Satan as we read about Creation and the Fall of Man. He was one of the closest angelic beings to God, and he came to believe himself worthy of God's throne. That said, it was his goal to tempt man, first through Adam and Eve, into doing the same thing, though they didn't realize that was what they were doing at the time:

> Now the serpent was more crafty than any of the wild animals the Lord God had made. He said to the woman, "Did God really say, 'You must not eat from any tree in the garden'?" The woman said to the serpent, "We may eat fruit from the trees in the garden, but God did say, 'You must not eat fruit from the tree that is in the middle of the garden, and you must not touch it, or you will die.'" "You will not certainly die," the serpent said to the woman. "For God knows that when you eat from it

your eyes will be opened, and you will be like God, knowing good and evil." When the woman saw that the fruit of the tree was good for food and pleasing to the eye, and also desirable for gaining wisdom, she took some and ate it. She also gave some to her husband, who was with her, and he ate it. (Genesis 3:1–6)

The kingdom of our enemy is earth, and the first man and woman were deceived into believing the lie that God was withholding something from them; that His provision was inadequate. In the moments before Eve believed that the fruit of the tree was good for food, we can only imagine her thoughts:

- Doesn't God want us to be knowledgeable of the earth? Why shouldn't we know of good and evil?

- God is good, so why does He not want us to be like Him?

- Does He not love us as much as we thought?

Of course, these are speculated questions, but the truth is that something entered her mind that caused her thinking to shift; suddenly, it became apparent to her that the fruit was not a bad thing as God had said. She was fully convinced of the lie, and it became a concrete belief. Without the slightest doubt in her mind, as far as we can tell, Adam and Eve proceeded to break through the single barrier God had placed before them for their protection.

Satan deceived them into what we know as sin, which is the act of putting our own self-interest above the command of God; it is disobedience centered around a greater love for self than for God. This was Satan's plan in light of his own failed attempt to succeed the throne of God. Although he was cast from Heaven, his vindication was, and will always be, to spite God by exploiting the desires of our flesh and tempting us into sin.

There is no greater demonstration of his hatred for God than persuading you to act in disobedience.

He thrives in causing God pain and is invigorated by complacency, groundless fear, isolation, confusion, and countless other things, which all stem, in one way or another, from his hatred for having been defeated. It all leads back to his ever-present lust for the throne of God, and this is what motivated him to build upon the foundation of Adam and Eve's sin. Since that day, he has been sowing seeds and investing in his kingdom.

Yes, our enemy has a kingdom in the same way we speak of the kingdom of God. He has a purpose for your life as does God. Our goal, as Christians, is to make Heaven a bigger place. Satan's goal is to make it smaller. He is no fool; he has read the end of the Bible, too, and he knows that he will ultimately lose, but the truth is this: he will still take winnings. Let me say that again, but in a different way. God and Satan are at war, but they are also in a race. In this race there will be a clear winner and a loser, but the loser will take home winnings in the form of every person who never called upon the name of Jesus as their Lord and Savior. Satan knows that the more he is able to hold you and me back from pursuing God's kingdom, the greater his potential winnings become. It's that simple. The more Satan can keep us from actively advancing God's kingdom, the more we will passively advance that of the lesser king.

Reflection Questions

- How has sin affected my life and those I love?
- Do I trust in the authority of God?

5

TEMPTATION

Satan plants seeds to grow his kingdom. One way he does this is through various temptations. These can be subtle or obvious, inactive or active, and they can be passive or aggressive. In the case of Christ as written by the disciple Matthew, the temptations were clear as day, and Jesus was required to look the enemy in the eyes and make an actionable decision:

> Then Jesus was led by the Spirit into the wilderness to be tempted by the devil. After fasting forty days and forty nights, he was hungry. (Matthew 4:1)

To provide some context for this story, Jesus was in the wilderness fasting in preparation to begin His ministry. There was never a more crucial time for the enemy to show up in His life. I don't believe that Satan has the ability to see outside of time the way God does, but rather, on a linear timeline like you and me, which means that he has to be watching us very closely to know when to tempt us in the most appropriate times.

Underline it, highlight it, or do whatever it is you need to do to remember this point: Satan cannot see what you will achieve for the kingdom of God, but he can see when you start taking your purpose seriously.

He can see when your spirit catches a breath of fresh air. He can see joy and seasons of vulnerability. When Jesus was about to begin His ministry, the enemy was afraid of the impact He was going to have on the world. The same is true in your life. You were born for a reason. You have a place on this earth. You belong somewhere in this uniquely imperfect web of joy and hardship, of togetherness and of emptiness.

Your ministry is to breathe and to be thankful; to give God glory with each step and every thought that enters your mind. The love that Christ has for you is to be multiplied in your heart and shared with the broken, because you were once in their shoes and remember how it was to feel that way. Your ministry is to live intentionally and in a way that points others to Jesus whether your words are directed or unspoken.

We are to be a city on a hill, Jesus said (Matthew 5:14), and we are to follow in His footsteps in the times when the enemy advances.

When Jesus was about to begin His ministry, Satan knew greatness would follow with every step the Messiah took. So he took action, and he did it at a time when Jesus would have been vulnerable and the most susceptible to being deceived; He had been fasting for forty days and nights, and was physically weaker than He had ever been:

> The tempter came to him and said, "If you are the Son of God, tell these stones to become bread." (Matthew 4:3)

Notice that the enemy's first words were mockery. What he said could also be paraphrased as this: "If you are the Son of God (as you claim to be), then prove it." Satan tempted Jesus to demonstrate His power, but Jesus knew that this would mean neglecting the purpose of His fast, which was to rely not on physical food, but on spiritual food through a closeness with God. In preparation for His ministry, Jesus was fasting the physical elements of food in order to hear from God more clearly and submit to the power of God, but Satan wanted to tempt Jesus into relying on His own power. But notice how Jesus responded:

> Jesus answered, "It is written: 'Man shall not live on bread alone, but on every word that comes from the mouth of God.'" (Matthew 4:4)

What Jesus did was acknowledge that the Word of God is of utmost importance. By saying, "It is written," Jesus was submitting to the way God has defined Himself in the Bible. Effectively, the point was that no matter what temptation comes our way, our very first call to action is to pit that temptation against the Word of God. This means we must study the Word until it is the filter through which we see the world.

We must know the Holy Spirit and awaken daily with a sense of fearlessness as men and women who will see the enemy's schemes as they are. Temptation and sin will not hold us down so long as we live submitted to the Holy Spirit, which is the same spirit who raised Christ from the dead and lives in us (Romans 8:11). The enemy hates you because God has chosen you as His beloved prize. And he hated Jesus because Jesus came to set you free from the curse of sin and death that Adam and Eve fell subject to.

You see, the temptation of Christ in that forest can be equated to the serpent's temptation of Adam and Eve in the Garden of Eden. In both instances, the tempted were marked with new beginnings. Adam and Eve walked with God in the garden and spent time in intimate community with Him just as Jesus did in the seclusion of the forest. But whereas they failed and fell into sin, Christ surpassed the schemes of the devil in order to ultimately fulfill His purpose on the cross, which was to pay the price for Adam and Eve's mistake.

Christ was tempted in three ways, and the first was a test of His own authority. The second temptation was designed for Jesus to put God's authority to the test:

> Then the devil took him to the holy city and had him stand on the highest point of the temple. "If you are the

Son of God," he said, "throw yourself down. For it is written: 'He will command his angels concerning you, and they will lift you up in their hands, so that you will not strike your foot against a stone.'" Jesus answered him, "It is also written: 'Do not put the Lord your God to the test.'" (Matthew 4:5–7)

In the second temptation, Satan, again, made a mockery of God. This time it was by twisting Scripture into a message that fit his end goal. Satan was trying to confuse Christ by putting a false sense of faith into His mind. Whether or not it is true that God would command His angels concerning the safety of Jesus is unimportant; what matters is what Jesus demonstrated with His response: that we are to trust our Father fully and without condition, never making decisions because we trust that God will come to our rescue.

God is faithful, but He also gave each of us the power of discernment and commands us to use it. He doesn't want us to make random choices, walk down the path of least resistance, or put God's faithfulness to the test by acting recklessly. We are to take knowledge and apply it to create wisdom. This goes for all areas of life: emotionally, physically, and spiritually.

The enemy can tempt us into things which appear to be good on the outside. Satan brought about a scenario which Jesus might have been able to use to bring glory to God: taking a leap and proving God's faithfulness to catch

Him. But Jesus demonstrated that we are never to put God to the test.

So, the first temptation was a test of Christ's authority. The second was designed to cause Jesus to put God's authority to the test. The third test was to have Jesus submit to Satan's authority:

> Again, the devil took him to a very high mountain and showed him all the kingdoms of the world and their splendor. "All this I will give you," he said, "if you will bow down and worship me." Jesus said to him, "Away from me, Satan! For it is written: 'Worship the Lord your God, and serve him only.'" Then the devil left him, and angels came and attended him. (Matthew 4:9–11)

Authority was the foundation of all three temptations brought unto Jesus. That is no coincidence; it is the foundation of sin. When sinning against God, we are effectively saying, in whatever circumstance we are in, that our desire is of greater importance than God's. We are putting ourselves in a higher regard than God, seating ourselves in a throne above God, just as Satan attempted to do prior to being cast from Heaven. After tempting Adam and Eve and introducing sin into the world, Satan began to take those building blocks and continuously invest into his kingdom. How? By repeatedly tempting us (and all people) and taking as many "winnings" as possible while he can.

So what does Satan think of you? He thinks you're a

tool he can use to bring pain and grieving to God. Is he wrong? Sadly not. The way the enemy uses our fallen nature to hurt God's heart is something we will never be able to change; we have all fallen and will continue to fall short of the glory of God (Romans 3:23), but the way the enemy uses us can be limited by our understanding and encounter with Jesus and His death on the cross.

If we begin to understand the story of Jesus and His purpose on earth, and if we couple that truth with the acknowledgement of Satan's purpose on earth today, then we will keep our enemy's kingdom from advancing.

Reflection Questions

- When have I positioned my own desires above God's? How can I avoid doing so in the future?

- Have I ever put God's faithfulness to the test?

- Do I make it a daily practice to consider the enemy's schemes?

6

THE STAGES OF SIN & BAD HABITS

In chapter four, the case was made that the first error we commonly make with regard to our enemy is misunderstanding his image. The second most common mistake is not paying close enough attention to the effects of the enemy's temptation in our lives. It's easy to get so caught up in the motions of life that we don't regularly self-assess to see if certain areas of our lives are as healthy as they could be.

When considering sin, negative habits, and the enemy's lies, the following stages will help you decide the best approach to improvement. To introduce the concept, let's use a common trait that many of us can relate to: impatience. This is a negative behavior that exists on its own, yet it often sends toxic ripples when it hits the waters of reality. These are the three stages of impatience and how it can manifest in your life:

1. You don't recognize (or refuse to recognize) that you're impatient, so you don't see the toxic ripples.
2. You recognize that you're impatient, but you don't see the toxic ripples.
3. You believe impatience is part of who you are that can't be changed.

The first level is simple, and it boils down to one of two things: denial or ignorance. The thing is, it can actually be somewhat difficult to recognize that you're impatient until someone tells you directly. Even then, being chided in this way often creates frustration and denial, which in most cases only leads to further conflict. Being told, "You're so impatient," is typically not received in a way that excites change.

Conversely, if you surround yourself with people who avoid conflict or who don't necessarily push you to be a better friend, colleague, or spouse, then there is a good chance you haven't ever been told that you're impatient. This is the ignorance part of the first level.

If you're in doubt that impatience is a problem for you, do some self-assessment and then ask a friend or loved one who you trust to be honest with you. Then, I challenge you to actually listen to them. And remember: because you've asked them to give you their opinion, being argumentative is really not an option.

The second level is a bit trickier. You have recognized your impatience, but you haven't noticed the byproducts. While you may see other negative things happening in your life, you aren't tying them back to something concrete with a unified root system. Things like bitterness, anger, closed-mindedness, insensitivity, and many more, are all toxic ripples that can easily tie back to impatience. The way to address this level is similar to the first: through prayer, self-assessment, and the conviction of the Holy Spirit, you will identify the toxic ripples so that you have an added incentive to cut the roots out.

The third level is the most harmful, and by the same token can be the most difficult to overcome. I've seen so many people, including myself, who have believed a lie to the point of it becoming their truth:

- I'm just an impatient person.

- My father was impatient. His father was impatient. It's in my blood.

- I've been impatient for too long. I'll never be able to change.

These are infectious thoughts that take your mind captive. When considering the act of dying to your flesh (Romans 8:13) and getting rid of certain negative characteristics, it's easy to be tempted to avoid addressing them because they have been a part of you for so long; you can easily believe that there is no use trying. Or perhaps you notice the toxic ripple effect but have not had anyone in your life to keep you accountable.

Accountability is born through vulnerability. If you don't open up to anyone about the things slowing you down, then you're effectively a one-man army attempting to defend all directions on your own. I'm guilty of this. It's something I can write openly and honestly about because I struggle with it seasonally. Through my own trials, I have seen that the opposite of growth is often found in isolation from fellowship with God and other believers, and that my time in this isolated valley is only prolonged when I pray for deliverance and wait for God to act without taking any action of my own.

When I asked a mentor of mine how best to pray for patience, this is what he said:

> *Nathan, God is not going to snap His fingers and make you a patient person; He is going to give you opportunities to practice patience.*

The answer floored me. It was such a great reminder that our Father is a God of process. He is a clay-maker who molds us to be beautiful pottery (Isaiah 64:8) and a blacksmith who works out our imperfections to create armor that will withstand the fires of our enemy. But He doesn't snap His fingers and make it happen. If you see that a quality of yours is negatively affecting your life, submit it to God and He will teach you to work through it.

If you wake up each day with a mindset to live according to the spirit rather than the flesh (Romans 8), God will do a great work through you: a strong follower of Christ who is unafraid to recognize and address their shortcomings head-on.

But it doesn't stop there.

Consider your God-given strengths and the dreams He has put in your heart and assess your tendency to self-doubt. Where do you fall in the three stages as it pertains to believing that you aren't good enough to succeed? Next, find someone in your life, maybe a few people, and tell them what you've learned. They will be there to keep you accountable to the goals you set for yourself and also for the dreams God has given you.

It's much easier for the enemy to cause you to back-slide when you're the only one who knows where you are on your journey. The people in your life who know and love you are the ones who are willing to remind you of your purpose. They want you to succeed as much as you want it for yourself, and they will be with you throughout the process for as long as you allow them to be.

While in the mindset of self-assessment, also call into consideration the areas of life where sin is evident, using the three stages as a guideline. Are you in stage three, having accepted the sin as being a part of you that can't be changed? Or are you in stage two, cognizant of the sin but not seeing the toxic byproducts? Perhaps you aren't immediately noticing a specific area where sin is manifesting in your life. If so, that's great. But just humor me and consider if you could be in the first stage where 1) something has plainly gone unnoticed or 2) you're in denial that a particular sin is present in your life.

I can't say enough how important it is for us to constantly be calling ourselves into question, never allowing our flesh to convince us that we're perfect and needing nothing in terms of improvement. God desires humility and a mind open to reflection and change. He wants us to be willing to let the Holy Spirit guide and convict us when things are a bit different than we perceive them to be.

Lastly, He wants us to lean on His Word. This ultimately speaks to the third stage of the enemy's plan for your sin, bad habits, or feeling of inadequacy. In Psalm 119:9–16, King David is writing a plan of action for staying on the path of purity. We will visit this psalm closely in a later chapter, but let's consider the final verse now:

> I will delight in your decrees; I will not forget your word.
> (Psalm 119:16)

The word "forget" here means *to ignore* in the original language of Hebrew. Treat this as a call to action against the things you believe are a part of you that cannot be changed or defeated. There is no bad habit that God has not dealt with. There is no sin, past, present, or future, that

Jesus has not already died to prevent you from having to atone yourself.

Nothing can separate you from the love of God (Romans 8:39). You are spotless in the sight of God through the selfless acts of Jesus on the cross, and you can let the weight fall from your shoulders as that reality sinks in. God loves you with everything in Him. You are not the person the enemy would have you believe you are.

Satan hates you because God has chosen you and because he lusts after the throne of God to this day. If he can't have it, he'll do everything he can to prevent you from achieving greatness for the kingdom of God. Ultimately, what he wants is for you to fall into complacency, isolation, hopelessness, envy, or any of the other feelings that stem from believing you are inadequate to succeed. These feelings directly advance the kingdom of our enemy by the simple fact that they don't allow you to live for God wholly and effectively.

But you're here, looking deeper, rising to the challenge set before you. In the chapters to come we're going to put many of the unhealthy fruits of inadequacy on trial so that we can work towards uprooting them from our lives.

Reflection Questions

- Do I make it a regular practice to call my flesh into question?

- How often do I expect results without the process?

- Am I truly vulnerable with anyone in my life?

PART II

THE FRUIT SYSTEM

So far, this book has been dedicated to understanding the root system that forms the foundation of feeling inadequate. Now, it's time to look closer at the toxic byproducts of believing the lie that you aren't good enough to impact the kingdom of God. Your impact includes small actions, great steps of faith, and everything in between.

The lie that you are not good enough to achieve what God has put in your heart does not affect just one single area of your life. It reacts like a firework, igniting in a central location and sending embers to activate many different places. This is the way of our enemy. He uses singular events or thoughts to create broadening wounds that have the potential to cause harm for long periods of time.

Here's the important thing to notice about Satan's lies: the broader the aftermath he creates in you, the greater the positive effect on his kingdom. This goes back, again, to the idea that we passively advance Satan's purpose for the world when we aren't actively pursuing the kingdom of God. The more we are held back from advancing the Gospel, serving our local church, speaking life into colleagues, friends, loved ones, and strangers, the more we are passively advancing Satan's plan, which is for the lost to remain lost, confused, and left to pay a debt that Jesus already lifted through His death on the cross.

So in what ways are we held back, exactly? What unhealthy fruits am I talking about?

Fruits can be good or bad, sweet or tart, and of all shapes, sizes, and colors. They are the product of the nutrients that a tree is taking in; they are an indication of good health. Jesus said that a good tree produces good fruit and a bad tree produces bad fruit (Matthew 7:18), though this is not to say that the bad fruits have an ugly appearance any more than we can say that Satan is a red, horned beast with a pitchfork.

The analogy of a tree and fruit used in Scripture is simply meant to point out that if a tree is nurtured, then it is going to be healthy. If a good tree is fed and watered, it will be strong and difficult to chop down, and the same is true for a bad tree. The more that sin and lies enter into your root system, the more bad fruits are produced. Unhealthy fruits.

In the chapters to come, we are going to look at seven different unhealthy fruits that I'm confident you have seen produced in your life at some point. Before we dive into those, let's look briefly at the most common example of fruits found in Scripture.

The Fruits of the Spirit

In this analogy, the Apostle Paul writes to all of us who call ourselves followers of Christ and who are led by the Holy Spirit. The tree he speaks of is you, yourself, and the fruits are the evidence that the Holy Spirit of God is the guiding force in your life. First, Paul sets the stage by demonstrating that our "flesh" and the "Spirit of God" are different entities, both desiring different things:

> So I say, walk by the Spirit, and you will not gratify the desires of the flesh. For the flesh desires what is contrary to the Spirit, and the Spirit what is contrary to the flesh. They are in conflict with each other, so that you are not to do whatever you want. But if you are led by the Spirit, you are not under the law. The acts of the flesh are obvious: sexual immorality, impurity and debauchery; idolatry and witchcraft; hatred, discord, jealousy, fits of rage, selfish ambition, dissensions, factions and envy; drunkenness, orgies, and the like. I warn you, as I did before, that those who live like this will not inherit the kingdom of God. But the fruit of the Spirit is love, joy, peace, patience, kindness, goodness, faithfulness, gentleness and self-control. Against such things there is no law. Those who belong to Christ Jesus have crucified the flesh with its passions and desires. (Galatians 5:16–24)

There are countless human characteristics or behaviors which demonstrate that actions bear fruit. Things like laziness, generosity, boredom, and pity. The idea that what you do produces results is so ingrained into our daily lives that it's impossible to go a day without noticing it. As Paul wrote to the Galatians, fruits are the consequences or by-products of the things we do.

Satan has a tendency to act as a coach. Like a play on a clipboard, he introduces a lie, then puts you in the game in hopes that you will play under the influence of that lie. What you do in the game is ultimately your decision; when you run, when you slow up, when you sprint, when you give up—the decision is yours. The fruits, then, are the byproducts of your decisions.

So what are the bad ones, what I call the "unhealthy fruits"? The ones we will look at are stagnancy, self-deprecation, distractedness, anger, sadness, shame, and envy. Each of these can very easily stem from the lie that you are unable to play an adequate role in advancing the kingdom of God. As you read through each unhealthy fruit, my prayer is that you will begin to fully recognize the harm in believing you are not good enough.

STAGNANCY

Imagine a man at sail in the middle of the ocean. There is no land in sight, though he is in search of a new place to live; somewhere he can begin the life he always hoped to find for himself. A life of purpose. What does he need in order to sail across the ocean? Just a boat, right? A vessel that floats with sails to catch the wind. Does it matter what size the boat is, or the material it is made of?

What does the captain need to look like or talk like in order to fulfill the dream in his heart? If he was once a drunk, a liar, or a thief, would it change anything? Would his past make any difference in his pursuit? Maybe it took the man ten years even to consider chasing his dream. Would that change the fact that all he needs to cross the ocean is a boat?

Imagine it's you in the ship and think about something God has placed in your heart. Whether that thing seems big or small, call it to the front of your mind. Now, have you ever been in a place spiritually, mentally, or emotionally where it seems like there is no wind in your sails? Like you aren't moving forward or backward, but just sitting still? That's stagnancy.

As the captain of a ship, this is a terrifying reality. Becoming stranded in the ocean with no wind has caused many boatmen to perish throughout the course of human history. In the moment when a captain recognizes that the wind has let up and his sails have fallen flat, no other thing in the world matters. His past is irrelevant. His socioeconomic status is unimportant. Any mistake he has made or failure that has befallen him could not be more ridiculous to dwell on. In that moment, the only thing worth chasing is another draft of wind. Large or small, whatever he can capture to gain momentum.

The dictionary defines stagnancy as "characterized by lack of development, advancement, or progressive movement" or "inactive, sluggish, or dull."

When I was considering writing this book, this was one of the first "unhealthy fruits" I identified. Stagnancy in my relationship with Christ has been something I've recognized frequently over the last several years, but somehow, I've allowed myself to slip back into it like any other bad habit. Perhaps you can identify with this.

There are many reasons we find ourselves stagnant from time to time, whether as a result of sin, shame, or uncertainty, but commonly I see this fruit being produced after we buy into the lie that we aren't capable of making a tangible, lasting impact on the world. Once this type of negative thinking becomes a habit, it is given the breeding ground it needs to thrive. And remember, the healthier the tree, the harder it is to take down.

To be totally transparent, I've probably thought some version of "I can't do this" a hundred times throughout the process of writing this book. Isn't it strange that God would inspire me to write a book about overcoming the feeling of inadequacy when I battle it daily? Isn't it strange that God would use a person like me, who has struggled with inadequate self-worth and confidence, to play this role in advancing the kingdom?

It's really not strange if we think about God's heart. Remember what He did with the loaves of bread and fish: He took what appeared to the disciples to be less than enough and multiplied it for His glory. You see, it wasn't ever about the amount of resources, but about perspective. It was about reframing Philip and Andrew's thought process in a way that made room for God to demonstrate His faithfulness to those who show up with what they have.

It's not always an easy thing to overcome the lies that cause us to become stagnant in our faith, but recognizing the significance of our decision not to fight is the first step in the battle. Make it a habit to remind yourself daily that we have an enemy who is very real, and his purpose for your life is that it would be of as little significance to God's kingdom as possible. The enemy's plan has not changed, but be encouraged that neither has God's desire to redeem His creation and use imperfect people to achieve greatness.

Remember how He took Moses on a journey to deliver the Israelites from captivity when Moses, himself, was captive to fear and shame as a fugitive? God is doing a similar work in me as I write these very words. What better way to help others overcome the feeling of inadequacy than to teach me to overcome it myself? He is molding me in this process so that you and I can relate to one another.

He wants you to know that you aren't alone in this battle against the enemy and the falsehoods that have been created in your life. The truth is, there is nothing in this world you can't do if God has called you to it. Just as a captain chases the next wind to the ends of the earth, if he has to, we must do whatever is necessary to put one foot in front of the other in our relationship with Christ and the dreams God has put in our hearts.

No one has ever achieved anything for the kingdom of God and wished they had walked when God asked them to run. No one has ever tried to help a lost person find hope in Jesus and wished they had waited a few more years to memorize more Scripture. Go out in faith and allow the Holy Spirit to act as your guide in those conversations. You may not have all the answers, but your answers are not what changes a person's heart in the first place (John 6:44a).

Movement is essential when it comes to the call of God, especially in the times when it doesn't make complete sense. Our flesh doubts by design, but don't ever allow yourself to think that there is something wrong with you for doubting God. Without the ability to question, without uncertainty, there can be no faith. Your tendency to doubt can actually turn into the greatest testament to your faith in God.

This book-writing process has not been an easy journey, but it has surprised me. Every time the enemy puts infectious thoughts in my head—the ones that say that no one will pick this book up or that I'm not going to add value to anyone's life—every time those thoughts enter my mind, I feel in my spirit to keep pressing on. Time is going to pass anyway, so I would rather try and fail for the kingdom of God than wonder about what might have been.

The more I'm tempted to believe I'm not good enough to succeed, the more I'm reminded that stagnancy is about so much more than the goals we set for ourselves and our ability to step towards the calling of God in our lives. It's about our pursuit of God in general. The lies the enemy puts in our head can have a profound impact on our prayer life, the time we spend in Scripture and worship, and our involvement in the community or church. And, if we're honest, falling into sin is easier when we're sitting still.

So where are you? Are you moving forward, backward, or are you standing still in your relationship with Christ? If backward, how quickly are you moving? If forward, are you moving in leaps and bounds? If you are standing still, how long have you been there?

The first step towards putting the unhealthy fruit of stagnancy to death is acknowledging its presence. Once you see that it's there, reconsider what you have read up until this point about the enemy and why he wants you to fail. And remember: if we are not actively advancing the kingdom of God, we are passively advancing the kingdom of our enemy.

You must take a serious look at the ways in which the enemy has held you back and take action against the lies that have prevented you from sailing. Only then will you find the freedom that allows God to use you for the things He has called you to. And believe me, if you are living and breathing, God has something He wants you to do with your life.

You are special and loved and sought after. Your past does not define you, and the wind can return to your sails just as soon as you recognize that it isn't there and you lift your eyes to Jesus. The enemy has lied to you before, but the truth found in God does not change. Satan's strategies have been the same since the temptation of Adam and Eve, and it's time you and I work towards breaking them down.

So if the first step to overcoming stagnancy is acknowledgement, the second is vulnerability. Whether God has put a specific calling in your heart at this moment or not, you need someone in your life who knows your goal to battle stagnancy. It doesn't matter if you don't have the perfect action plan to share with a friend. It just matters that you open up and tell them that you're trying to get there.

Allowing someone in your life to know that you recognize your importance in advancing the kingdom of God is vital for the days when you forget it yourself. Because those days, as I'm sure you are already aware, are not hard to come by. In fact, those days can easily become weeks and months, even years, before we realize what has happened. Don't be afraid to tell someone that you don't have it all together. Don't pretend to be put together for the sake of reputation, because the kingdom of God does not care about any of that.

And please, more than anything, don't allow yourself to feel guilty if you have been stagnant. Shame is not from God; it is another tool of the enemy to twist the convictions of our loving Father. Shame would have you believe that God is upset with you for having wasted time. Friends, that is not the way God operates. We don't see Him shame Moses for the years he spent as a fugitive. Instead, we see Him take something stagnant and give it momentum. He gave Moses purpose and a mission that required great faith, and it required leaning on the strength and power of God. But the best part is what God did next. After giving Moses purpose, He sent him to the Israelites to build and foster relationships and accountability, both of which would be necessary to fulfill God's plan. God knew that the elders of the Israelites would stand behind Moses to make sure he would not fall back on the feeling that he was inadequate to succeed.

So first, we acknowledge stagnancy. Next, we communicate the call of God on our lives to a friend willing to listen and stand by us. The third and final step, which should also be present in the midst of the first and second, is to spend intentional time in community with Jesus. There is no such thing as a fruitful calling without Jesus in the center of it. By His stripes we are healed from sin, and by His scars we are redeemed and worthy of the fullness of life.

Each one of the unhealthy fruits we discuss in these chapters is going to involve Jesus in some capacity. Nothing broken becomes whole without the involvement of Him who was first broken and made new for you, and for me. Nothing imperfect becomes clean except through Jesus, who bore the weight of every imperfection of mankind and put each of them to death by His own blood. Jesus is the way, the truth, and the life (John 14:6). He is all we need.

Reflection Questions

- Am I moving forward, backward, or standing still in my relationship with Christ?

- What does growth mean to me?

8

SELF-DEPRECATION

You are probably still reading this book because you have, at some point, felt like you were not qualified to do something for the kingdom of God. But have you ever felt that you are *disqualified* from fulfilling your calling because of who you are or because of your weaknesses?

Have you ever felt insignificant? I have. In fact, I can't remember many days that I have woken up with an overwhelming sense of worth and confidence that I'm everything Jesus says I am. Seeing this tendency in myself led me to realize that I've enabled the enemy to work on the destruction of others because I've been doing his job so well in my own life. That is ultimately what self-deprecation creates.

Believing that we can't succeed in impacting God's kingdom is bad enough, but compounding that with a hyper focus on our flaws is poison to the soul. Comparison to others is a huge part in this—amplifying what we see wrong with ourselves by obsessing over the image of what we believe we ought to be like. We do this with our physical appearance often, but it can happen with our spiritual lives as well. I used to see men spiritually lead their wives in ways I hadn't yet figured out, and I immediately began to believe I was less of a man. And it was especially unhealthy because it caused me to be less confident in the things I did well in my household. My shortcomings became my only focus, and I projected them onto other areas of life as a result.

In the same way as stagnancy, the first step in overcoming self-deprecation is realizing that you struggle with it. It's important to frequently take a step back and examine your spiritual, emotional, and mental life, and it's important to have people in your life who can check on you and call you out when they see an inconsistency in how you're acting and the way God has called you to act.

The second step is to see yourself the way God sees you. This is what Moses had to do when he was called to return to Egypt and confront Pharaoh. Remember, Moses's first inclination was to ask, "Who am I that I should go to Pharaoh and bring the Israelites out of Egypt?" Moses believed that he was disqualified from participating in God's work because of his imperfections and past mistakes. He was in a place where his *identity* was determined by his *weaknesses*, and he was operating from the assumption that God requires perfection.

Remind yourself this week that God knows you aren't perfect, yet he has called you. He loves you so intensely that

He gave His only Son to die for you (John 3:16) and that you are no longer an orphan, but have a Father who loves you with a love that never ends (John 14:18).

Be kinder to yourself. Jesus didn't give us freedom so that we could spend it putting ourselves down.

In Proverbs chapter 5, King Solomon wrote arguably one of the most popular verses in Christianity; I'm certain you have heard it, though you may not have considered it in the context of self-deprecation:

> Trust in the Lord with all your heart, and do not lean on your own understanding. Acknowledge him in all your ways, and he will make straight your paths. (Proverbs 3:5–6)

Is it not true that we have an "understanding" or "perception" of ourselves that, from time to time, becomes different than God's? When our Father sees a weakness in us, He does not have the same thought processes as we do. His understanding of shortcomings, bad habits, and the twisting turns of life is opposite ours, and is always focused on growth and redemption over shame and frustration. He does not dwell on our negative characteristics the way we do; instead, He sees the process of growth the way we see the sunrise every morning, each day presenting a new opportunity for positive change. Friends, He is good, and His love for you is unending. Each day should be spent trying to become more and more like Jesus, and this begins in your heart. If you have acknowledged that something you feel is holding you back from your pursuing the kingdom of God, or that something you feel disqualifies you from being engaged with God's purpose for your life, now is the time to come up with a plan of action. In the same way that we should pray for opportunities to practice patience, we ought to be praying for opportunities to grow—situations that force us out of our comfort zones.

It's uncomfortable, terrifying even, but it's a necessity.

For example, if God has called you to pastor people from a stage, don't be discouraged or ashamed if nerves get the best of you initially; take ownership of your calling and pray for more opportunities to practice. God will provide them, I can promise you that. Will you mess up a few times? Probably. But in the end, what do we really have if not the courage to step out in the times that make us vulnerable to failure? Let Him grow your faith. Give Him the opportunity to multiply your offering the way He did in the five loaves and two fish story.

Remember, God's desire is for you to show up with what you have and allow Him to do a great work through you. We are vessels for the Gospel of Christ, but for a boat to sail it must first be in the water.

Reflection Questions

- Do I have goals for my personal development? Am I the only one who knows what they are?

- Do I have a mentor who I can meet regularly to help me focus on progress?

9

DISTRACTEDNESS

We live in a world of instant gratification and we're constantly looking for new ways to be relieved from the issues we face. Whether these are issues at work, at home, with friends, or in the community, there seems to be no shortage of problems that fight for our attention. What I would like to submit to you is that allowing "God dreams" to gather dust in the corner of our minds is an issue that should be at the top of our list to address.

I believe that is why many of you are here, reading this book, whether you realized it when you picked it up or not: you know that you are alive for a reason, but perhaps you have become distracted in your pursuit because you bought into the lie that you are not good enough to succeed in God's kingdom.

Now, I'm not going to be addressing specific hobbies or activities, because that isn't what is important. You know what yours are, and I know what mine are. What I'm encouraging you to do is *consider* if any of those hobbies have become an excuse for spending less time pursuing your calling due to the fear of uncertainty or failure.

Using me as an example, I began asking myself recently if the things I invest time in doing (e.g., rock climbing) had become an excuse for spending less time writing, which I knew I had been called to. The answer was yes, and that answer did two things in my heart: it surprised me, and it made me feel guilty.

First, the surprise. The thing about forcing ourselves to dig deep and ask difficult questions is that God will most definitely reward this effort by revealing what we haven't considered. I felt that my writing was weak, not relatable, and uninteresting, but I was afraid to seek guidance and critique even though I knew God had called me to writing. So I spent time rock climbing and found ways to validate the pastime so that I didn't have to acknowledge the fact that I was *avoiding my role in the kingdom of God.*

Next was the feeling of guilt. It was not actually caused by the answer God gave me, but by the result of believing that I had failed Him. So the full progression was 1) believing that I was not good enough, to 2) being distracted, and to 3) feeling that I had taken the calling of God for granted, which fed right back into the feeling of not being good enough.

If you have ever been caught in that toxic cycle, or if you are in that place now, you know it's not a great feeling.

During these times, the primary truth to remember is that guilt is not from God. We are prompted by the Holy Spirit to make various changes in our lives, but the feelings of guilt and shame are from our enemy. Secondly, we have to remember that God is our Father who loves us and wants us to grow, develop, and replicate our wisdom in other believers. Because how can we help others through these circumstances if we have never gone through them ourselves?

What we do with distractedness is find the things that are directly tied to the act of avoiding our God-given dreams and focus on them. I love rock climbing and don't intend to stop altogether, but I now see that the reasons I was using to justify this hobby pale in comparison to the eternal benefit of allowing God to take me out of my comfort zone and into my purpose.

Are various pastimes the only way to be distracted? There are a number of dangers to the kingdom of God in this realm, and the other one I would like for you to consider is distracting opinions.

Everyone, it seems, has an opinion of what it means to be successful. There is no shortage of opinions from friends and family with regard to life, marriage, career sustainability, and countless other things, but we have to be careful to test everything against God's Word and the guidance of the Holy Spirit. The truth is, those who love you the most and want what is best for you don't always *know* what is best for you. This is not to say they are wrong in the advice they offer, but that everything—opinion, idea, prophecy, and encouragement—should be considered carefully and tested. Paul says this in the first book of Thessalonians:

> Don't stifle those who have a word from the Master. On the other hand, don't be gullible. Check out everything, and keep only what is good. Throw out anything tainted with evil. (1 Thessalonians 5:20–22 MSG)

In this passage, Paul is encouraging the Thessalonians to remain open-minded towards those who believe God has given them a prophetic word. At the same time, he is warning them against believing everything that is spoken to them. This is a reminder for each person reading Paul's letter to listen and act with reason and discernment, through the lens of God's Word, without making decisions based on the assumed character or intentions of the one offering prophecies.

In the same way, I believe Paul's encouragement applies to opinions offered from loved ones about the decisions you should or shouldn't make in life. Our loved ones have our best interest at heart, always, but sometimes their judgment may be clouded by fear.

Decisions like going to ministry school, moving across the world to be a missionary, being an artist or an author without a clear view of your financial future, and many others—there are thousands of ways God calls His children that seem foolish or reckless to loved ones, whether those loved ones are parents, grandparents, friends, teachers, or counselors.

These people love you like no one else and, for that reason, can easily become reluctant or blind to God's will for your life. At the same time, know this: God has put these people in your life to be a voice of wisdom in times when steps of faith are required. Each of us has the ability to question and doubt God, which allows faith to exist, and the same can be said of our human relationships. Distractions are created when we lean too heavily on what other people think and start down paths that may ultimately prolong our God-given purpose. So just as Paul encouraged the Thessalonians, listen to those who want to help you, but test everything you hear according to your personal relationship with God and with His Word.

Disclaimer for young people: you are to obey your parents, for this pleases the Lord (Colossians 3:30). There will come a time when you will make decisions for yourself. Be patient in the Lord and continue to grow; don't act rashly or in defiance of your mother, father, or parental figure. Learn from their decisions and use every breath you have been given to maximize your personal development, as this will help you succeed in God's plan for your life. Ultimately, because God has commanded you to obey your parents, your act of obedience is really to Him.

Reflection Questions

- Have I allowed a hobby to take the place of God's calling?

- How do the opinions of my loved ones affect me?

- How often do I compare the advice given me against the Word of God?

10

ANGER

Lord, thank you for considering me worthy to be a part of the king-
dom of God and to write this book for your glory. Thank you for
everything you do to provide for me and Stefanie. You have given us
more than we deserve. Lord, give me strength like only you can give.
I surrender my circumstances to you and will actively work to forgive
where forgiveness is needed, and I will lean on your promises in the
midst of my feelings of exhaustion. Lord, you have called me to some-
thing great; something greater than any other thing I could spend my
time doing right now. The impact that this book will have on people
will be greater than anything I have ever done before and is worth
every effort. I will not be a man who allows anger a foothold in my
life, and I will stay the course set before me. Thank you for your
patience with me in this process. Amen.

As I'm sure you know, bitterness and anger are not hard to
come by in some seasons of life. While writing this book, I
had several events in my life that caused bitterness to be
harbored in my heart. I was frustrated, easily distracted, and
was beginning to slip back into the fear of not being good

enough to complete this book. The above is a prayer I wrote down after an emotional "brain dump" in a journal of mine. During the time spent in prayer, I was reminded that I have more than I deserve and really don't have much room to complain.

God is *allowing* me to be a part of this journey and is simply asking me to show up with what I have so that He can multiply my efforts as only He can.

So what do we do with anger? When life happens, how do we handle ourselves as followers of Christ? An easy assumption to make is that anger is a sin. The truth is, anger is not wrong in itself—it's what we do with it that matters. Paul says this in Ephesians:

> In your anger do not sin. Do not let the sun go down while you are still angry, and do not give the devil a foothold. (Ephesians 4:26–27)

When Paul says, "In your anger do not sin," he acknowledges that there are going to be times when we are angry and implies that we, in the midst of our anger, have the ability to decide what comes next. Nowhere does Paul say, "Do not ever be angry" or "Anger always leads to sin." Instead, he makes sure the Ephesians know that they always have a choice about what to do with their anger, no matter what the circumstance is or who is at fault.

You have probably noticed that a major theme in this book is mindfulness or awareness. The idea is this: the only way we put to death the unhealthy fruits of feeling inadequate is by acknowledging that the lie is there in the first place. Only then can the Holy Spirit guide us through our tendencies to be stagnant, distracted, or self-depreciating. Taking this idea broader, the way to understand the lie is to know who the liar is and what his goals are. That is why this book is structured the way it is.

We can't address anger and its consequences unless we first know why it is there in the first place and recognize that inaction allows it to fester and turn into sin, abuse, bitterness, malice, insensitivity, and so many other things.

What I realized after praying the prayer given at the start of the chapter is that God was allowing bitterness in my heart to remind me that pursuing Him is going to take choice and effort. Recall that the best way to pray about becoming a more patient person is not by asking God for patience, but by recognizing that God will send you opportunities to practice patience; after that, it's up to you. The same goes for anger. If you want to get rid of it, then you must live in expectancy for the Holy Spirit to prompt you when you're getting heated up.

He will nudge you quietly and say, "Hey, didn't you pray to get rid of anger? Make the choice to say something other than what your flesh wants to say, or just walk away." Your actions will show others that the Holy Spirit is at work in your life, as you will have demonstrated the sweet fruit of self-control.

But how can anger come from a false feeling of inadequacy? If this unhealthy fruit does not directly apply to you, keep reading anyway. An understanding of each of these seven unhealthy fruits is important for your role in the Body of Christ. That goes for the fruits of stagnancy, self-deprecation, distractedness, and the ones to follow. If you feel they don't apply to you right now, learn about them so that you can help a colleague, friend, or spouse work through the issues if they come to you for advice.

We were never meant to be alone. Adam was given a woman who would keep him company and who would also complement his abilities and strengths with those of her own. Your testimony is not the same as mine; I struggle with temptations that you don't, and vice versa, but ultimately that makes us stronger together and is even more of a reason for the enemy to isolate and keep us from community.

Now, if you think about the purpose God has for your life, it carries an enormous importance and significance. When God first called me to be a writer, it was fresh, clear, and gave me hope and excitement unlike anything I had ever felt before. By contrast, after the push and pull of the enemy's lies over several years, it was extremely disheartening to consider all the time I had spent dreaming and anticipating my purpose as a writer, only to believe I was not good enough to succeed in it. So when someone I know asked me why I hadn't ever shown them my writing or why

Anger

I hadn't published anything yet, can you guess the emotion that filled my heart first? That's right—anger. Anger towards myself and towards God for dangling a dream in front of my eyes that I would never reach. I've been so angry before that I would say things like this:

I can't even believe I thought I could do this. Look at how much time I've wasted. And for what? All of my friends and family know I've been writing for the last six years, and what do I have to show for it? A couple short stories and poems? I'm not an author and I'll never be.

Perhaps you understand this narrative well and you know that it's easy to lock up and hide the talent we believe God has given us. Because what if we're wrong? Vulnerability is not easy, and for most people it does not come naturally. "They can't hurt me if they don't see me," we find ourselves saying. But we were not created to go through life alone any more than we were created to go through life stagnant, self-deprecating, distracted, or angry.

Ask yourself how you can be more vulnerable today. And not only with a friend, but with God as well. The Holy Spirit's guidance will see you through anger if you allow Him to be involved. In the universe you have no greater advocate than God, but He can only help you as much as you will let Him in.

Reflection Questions

- Have I allowed anger or bitterness in my heart? Have I locked God out?
- Do I allow the Holy Spirit to guide me every day?

11

SADNESS

Similar to anger, sadness is not a bad thing in itself. In fact, sadness is the gateway of compassion found by looking through the lens of empathy and a common understanding of pain. It can be a beautiful thing, which allows us to express our emotions in a way that other people can identify with and connect to, but, like anger, it can be used in harmful ways and can evolve into deeper emotions and long-lasting seasons of pain and depression.

Each of us should maintain a healthy amount of sadness in our lives so that we don't miss the issues all around us, but what we do with sadness is the most important thing. It could be a catalyst for change in our lives or in the life of a stranger, or it could be the thing that drags us further into our own heads where nothing bright or true can find a way to flourish.

Let's think about Jesus for a moment. *Gratitude* is one of the first words that comes to mind when considering Jesus' death on the cross, but it's so much more than that.

When we consider the crucifixion, we're grateful in a way that is much different than being grateful for a meal, for having work, or for having a roof over our heads. That's because the feeling is combined with sadness for everything that Jesus went through—the lashings, the crown of thorns, the act of being nailed to a rugged, wooden cross to gasp for air until He took His final breath—we remember that Jesus was a man, and we feel a gratefulness that is so much stronger than any other ordinary feeling of thanks.

Take a moment and look at your own hands. Feel your palms in remembrance of the nails that pierced Christ's hands for you. Look at your feet and remember all the places you are able to walk and run by the grace of God through the acts of Jesus on that cross. Cup a hand to the side of your face the way Mary, mother of Jesus, wanted to as He was taken away to be beaten and crucified for crimes He did not commit.

My heart hurts for the people in Jesus' life who could do nothing to help Him. If you've ever felt helpless in the slightest way, or rejected, unloved, or unappreciated, then you can understand Christ in the slightest way as well. The more pain and hardship we have endured in this life, the more we are able to empathize with our Jesus.

Now let's look at another manifestation of sadness. Sadness as it relates to our place in the kingdom of God is the launchpad for something called powerlessness. It functions like anger does, in that it can be directly related to the importance we feel for the calling of God, which we have been unable to fulfill. It's the idea that "If I can't do this, then everything else is meaningless," a defeating all-or-nothing perspective. In other words, the lie of the enemy is this: if you fail at accomplishing the thing you were made to do, nothing else is worth doing.

If you or anyone you know has reached this point of powerlessness, urge them to remember the three stories you read in earlier chapters. Cling to these simple truths that God spoke through each one and that He speaks to you today:

- Bring what you have and I will supply the rest.

- If I have called you, then you are enough.

- I'm here with you. You have no reason to doubt.

Allow sadness to be the foundation of compassion and recognize it as a part of your testimony that you can use to impact the lives of others. There is arguably no other emotion more powerful and more vital to the advancement of the kingdom of God than empathy.

Reflection Questions

- In what ways can I empathize with Christ in His suffering?

- Have I allowed myself to feel powerless to overcome sin, weakness, or the enemy's lies?

- What are my self-destructive habits when allowing sadness to grow?

12

SHAME

God has forgiven me, but I can't forgive myself.

It's difficult to compartmentalize our feelings when it comes to sin. We are not accustomed to feeling the joy of God's forgiveness while at the same time moving on as if a sin was never committed. It has, for so long, been ingrained in our minds that actions should always have consequences.

Good things are rewarded and evil things are punished; yet we know, as followers of Christ, that a punishment has already been rendered for all the mistakes we will make for the rest of our lives. So what do we do with these conflicting standards? Typically, we combine them. We inflict our own sentence in the form of shame and guilt as an attempt to show remorse for our actions and to prove to God that we see what we have done.

This is so harmful. Not only can this spiral into isolation and hopelessness, but, more importantly, it means we believe that the sacrifice of Christ was insufficient. When we impose our own self-punishment for sinning against God, we are refusing grace and stripping the cross of its meaning.

Repentance in its purest form means a change of direction. After committing a sin, we are to recognize what we have done and make a choice to turn around and walk the other way in future circumstances. We are not, however, to be burdened by shame and remorse for our actions. Jesus died so that we would not have to pay the penalty for our immorality, not that we may continue on in sin, knowing that we have grace (Romans 6:15), but that we may recognize the incredible length that God is willing to go to for us to return to His arms.

It doesn't make sense. It's not fair, what Jesus went through on our behalf, but the truth is this: Jesus Christ, the Son of God, died so that you would have the opportunity to pursue righteousness *shamelessly*. He was crucified so that you would have access to the fullness of life found only in a pure relationship with God. Though sin still exists, and though it always will, Jesus has given you the chance to have ten thousand second chances, all while never once changing in the eyes of God. You were purchased at a high price. You have been redeemed. Now, today and tomorrow, you are to take up your cross, go and sin no more (John 8:11), and allow the heart of God into the dark places where shame and guilt have built strongholds.

In the book of Ephesians (verse 4:27), Paul wrote about preventing Satan from "getting a foothold." He is speaking about anger in that context, but a foothold has many applications. Giving this position to the enemy means giving him a place to balance and to rest; it means close contact between you and him.

Once the enemy is involved and you enter into a cycle of sin, then shame becomes like wearing a scarlet "A" under your shirt and constantly wondering if everyone can see it. You know the sin is there, and you begin to fear that others will find out. So you pull back. Either you keep conversation closer to the surface, or you stop being around as much.

Both are forms of isolation and, as you may know, will only make it harder for you to find healing. Just like Moses assumed he needed to be perfect to do God's work, we often pit ourselves against an unrealistic standard when it comes to being vulnerable about sin. We believe that everything in our lives must live up to a certain level of goodness before being broadcasted to others, even those closest to us.

Have you ever felt that you're the only one who doesn't "have it all together"? Or perhaps that you and your significant other are the only ones who fight? Shame hinders us from seeking accountability in others by creating the lie that no one else is "like us" or struggles with the things we struggle with. "They would not love me if they knew" and "They would not understand what I'm dealing with" are common misconceptions.

The feeling of inadequacy has a similar message. Whereas shame says, "I can't believe I did this," the feeling of inadequacy says, "I can't believe I'm not good enough to do this." Each lie creates the belief that we are less than God says we are, and each creates the atmosphere for our enemy to be given a foothold.

The false perception that we have to reach a level of perfection or expertise before being transparent about our God-given talents is a real thing created by fear of failure and the associated shame. But the truth is, though we have sin in our lives, our purpose to reflect God's light to the world has not changed since the beginning of time. Just because man fell to sin does not mean that our calling to bring glory to our Father was nullified. Instead, be reminded that we are now (each and every one of us) imperfect people who are called to broadcast whatever He has given us, even if it's a little messy at first.

It never ceases to amaze me how easy it is to backslide into hours or days of shameful, self-deprecating thoughts before realizing that it has been happening. So what is the action plan? Acknowledgement, first, as always, and then being intentional with your battle plan. As with impatience, distractedness, anger, and all of the other unhealthy fruits, the Holy Spirit is there to guide and prompt you to make the right choice.

But at the same time, a warrior must learn how to fight. The general of an army will create a defense strategy, but the soldiers must take up weapons and hold their lines. If we don't take action, the enemy will advance against us. No questions asked. And remember, if we are not taking action to advance the kingdom of God, we are passively advancing the kingdom of our enemy.

Do you think Moses felt ashamed after murdering the Egyptian slave driver who had abused the Hebrew woman? Absolutely. Over the years that followed the incident, that shame likely caused Moses to question everything he knew about himself. He fled Egypt and started a new life in hopes of forgetting the terrible things he had done, but in the back of his mind, I doubt he was ever able to forget. And his people? They were still suffering under Egyptian rule, and he had abandoned them.

In Moses' mind, these actions could have made him feel worthless and too damaged to use for good, but that is not how God viewed him. God sought Moses and commanded him to take up his sword in battle for the kingdom. He would no longer allow Moses to feel the weight of shame and live a life in fear and isolation, so He redeemed him and gave him purpose. Do you know what else? He demonstrated to Moses that, no matter how hard he was on himself, no matter how long he beat himself up for his past mistakes, nothing would heal him like knowing he had another chance at a life of purpose.

What about Peter? Do you think he felt ashamed after doubting Jesus in that storm? I would say more than likely. After being reminded to have faith, Peter might have returned to the ship and lay in bed all night reflecting on his journey with Christ and believing he had let Jesus down. Alternatively, he could have allowed that moment to fuel him to become closer to Christ and to be more intentional with his personal growth.

Reflection Questions

- How can I forgive myself today?
- How and when have I misunderstood the meaning of repentance?
- How often do I impose my own punishment for sin in the form of shame?

13

ENVY

In the midst of a culture that encourages material posses-
sion and normalizes the act of comparison, it's important
that we regularly visit this unhealthy fruit. We are constantly
surrounded by the "best side" of the people we see on so-
cial media, which tricks us into believing that their lives are
perfect all the time. The body of Christ is not safe from
comparison either. If you are involved with your local
church or have friends who are chasing after God, you may
have found yourself at some point wondering, "God, are
you going to use me like you're using them?" or "Why don't
I have more clarity regarding my purpose when it seems
like they do?" My point is, it can be just as easy to envy
intangible things—like closeness to God or spiritual impact—as it is material possessions. This can cause us to
assume we are not good enough in the eyes of God or that
He doesn't think we're ready yet.

To ensure we're on the same page, envy is not admiring
what someone else has; there is certainly a healthy way to
strive to be like the people we admire. Envy is the feeling

of discontentment when looking at aspects of another person's life and wishing they were our own. We live in a world full of choices, and there are so many different avenues to success that we can find ourselves wondering how our life would be had we done *this* or how much happier we would be if we were more like *them*.

Here's the way we combat envy: we listen to Jesus and pay close attention to His purpose on earth. In the Gospel of John, Jesus is said to have come "so that no person would hunger or thirst" (John 6:35). When we look at the original Hebrew text, we see that John was not referring to our physical needs, but to the needs of the human soul.

You see, we have this constant longing to be refreshed, strengthened, and supported, and when we don't look to Jesus for this need to be met, we chase the temporary pleasures of life. This is contrary to the purpose Jesus had in dying a sinner's death. Did you know that the same Hebrew word for "thirst" was used in Jesus' final moments on the cross?

> After this, Jesus, knowing that all things had already been accomplished, to fulfill the Scripture, said, "I am thirsty." (John 19:28)

We know that Jesus was physically thirsty, but could it be that He was also alluding to a deeper spiritual truth when breathing those three words? In taking the weight of our sin upon His perfect, sinless shoulders, Jesus suffered the most intense and inconceivable spiritual pain: being forsaken by God. In those desperate moments, His soul longed for something to refresh, strengthen, and support Him, but He was answered by God in the way that you and I deserve to be—with silence and abandon.

Jesus, the perfect Son of God, was left to die a sinner's death in order that you and I could live a life of freedom and a life to the fullest degree. This life we have been given is the only thing in this world worth envying.

The Son of God came so that none would ever have to thirst, so why do we constantly look for water in places that are only a temporary fix?

As you continue to press on in advancing the kingdom of God, don't look around at what others are doing; if you do, let it be to stay accountable and encouraged, but never to envy. God has given you breath in your lungs for a different reason than your neighbor, your mother and father, your siblings, your best friend, your pastor, your schoolteachers, your banker, your church friends, and so on. He has given you passions and skills that have a unique application to the kingdom. So as you look around and see what seems to be perfection in others, let it be a reminder to you that God sees you as perfect and complete through the selfless act of Jesus on the cross.

Reflection Questions

- How often do I compare myself to others as a means of validation?

- By contrast, how often do I seek the heart of God to discover what He thinks of me?

- When my soul needs to be refreshed, strengthened, and supported, am I looking to Jesus? If not, where am I looking?

PART III
THE GARDENER

What is a garden, and why does a garden need a gardener?

A garden is a designated place for different flowers and plants to be looked after, cultivated, and sustained. Unlike a mountain range or forest, gardens do not exist naturally; they are intentionally built and maintained for a specific purpose, whether that is to grow food or to create an atmosphere of peace and tranquility.

Gardens are created, like you and me.

That said, without a gardener, a garden would be unable to fulfill the reason it was brought into existence. Stones are laid carefully but easily become overgrown by unkempt grass; vines spread and suffocate everything in their path, leaving the beauty of a garden tarnished; weeds cover the surface of the ground and distract from the main focal points.

In the introduction to Part I: The Root System, I asked you to begin thinking about areas of your life that could be seen as weeds in a garden. After reflecting on each of the toxic fruits we examined in the last seven chapters, my prayer is that your eyes have now been opened to the full extent of Satan's plan for the lie of inadequacy in your life.

Now, my prayer is that you would seek the heart of God with everything in you and cling to Him as our Gardener, for He is good.

14

THE GARDEN

God made Adam and Eve beautiful and perfect, lacking in nothing, and He provided them with every nutrient they needed to thrive. They were allowed to eat from every tree but one, drink from every source of water, and they walked in step with God so that their spirits were always in tune with Him. God was their Master Gardener and wanted them to have everything they needed to grow, to be fruitful, and to bring glory to His name.

Despite sin entering the world, Adam and Eve were still the beautiful creations of God, and despite the many mistakes we have ever made, we remain His workmanship, purchased at the high price of Christ's death on the cross. The desire of God's heart is to tend to every area of our lives like a gardener who *uproots* unhealthy plants and establishes new ones in their place.

You and I are gardens created by God to live out His will. Adam was created from the dust of the earth, and Eve was created from Adam. In making Adam and Eve, the

Creator of the Universe repurposed the things He had already brought into existence and gave them a purpose unlike any of the other creatures He had made.

Even when we appear to be in the worst condition of our lives, even when we're tattered and broken by sin or being sinned against, nothing will ever change the fact that we were created out of intention. No matter what you feel or the lies told to you by the enemy, you are the craftsmanship of a God who acts not out of flippancy or amusement, but out of purpose.

What I know to be true is this: you and I are here. The world is both broken and breaking all around us and is in a constant state of turmoil. We are in a season of existence unlike any other before us, and it is our responsibility to find our place in it. Whether the things we do in this life seem small or large in the grand scheme of things, every action we make to propel the kingdom of God echoes throughout Heaven and resounds like a mighty drum in the ears of our enemy.

That is why we need God to tend to us—because of the ever-present battle against our bodies, minds, and spirits. If we open our eyes to the fact that we have an enemy who wants to destroy everyone we love, we must then be prepared to take a stand against him.

The reality of our world is that, while we may not know exactly when, we know that it will come to an end. For that reason, it is paramount that we take a serious look at our lives and identify what holds us back from advancing God's kingdom. You have a unique purpose, and that means there is a unique strategy against you.

So what do you do first? You take charge, and you do it boldly. Jesus did not die so that you would live confined by the lie that you are not good enough to succeed.

Believe this today: you are good enough. Inadequacy is in us all and will always be present when we are chasing after something God never intended for us to do without His involvement. Take action against the enemy's grip on your life and maintain your gaze on the One who gives life abundantly. Find accountability and be transparent and vulnerable. If God has called you to something specific, tell someone about it so that they can remind you when you forget or are tempted to believe God never really told you it to begin with.

Allow God to tend to the garden that makes up every fiber of who you are and who you want to become. Take a stand against the enemy daily. Never ever forget how easy it can be to passively advance Satan's kingdom. Make it a point to overcome the obstacles in front of you now that you recognize them for what they are.

As with Philip, God has already given us everything we need to win. Moses was deemed good enough, despite his failures, as are you, and God does not require you to be perfect any more than Jesus expected Peter to stand atop the water on his own.

Still, the enemy can creep into our heads and tempt us to doubt. We know that the devil has come to steal, kill, and destroy (John 10:10), and we must remember that, in the midst of every good thing to do with God and His kingdom, the enemy is there believing the opposite for your life and plotting against you.

He does this, as we've learned, by instilling stagnancy, self-deprecation, distractedness, bitterness, anger, isolation, hopelessness, sadness, shame, and envy in our hearts. He seeks to withhold the truth from us, which is God's truth that Jesus came to offer the gift of salvation and a life of spiritual opportunity and purpose, which he knows will provide a feeling of fulfillment unlike anything the world can offer.

Still, that would not stop the enemy from dangling the sweet-seeming things of the world in front of our eyes. Be reminded that the more you chase after God's kingdom, the more the enemy begins to fear your success. Temptation is your way of knowing that you are feared. And remember: the feeling of inadequacy is evidence that the enemy of God has acknowledged your potential. That is one of the most important statements I pray you will take to heart. Put it on your refrigerator or mirror—somewhere you will see it daily to be reminded that you are important and that the devil knows it.

We will not be people who covet the lives of others. We will seek contentment in Christ for the things we have and for the purpose put in our hearts. We will pursue God with everything we have, because that is what He asks of us (Matthew 22:37). We will take up our swords daily and battle with the enemy because we acknowledge that he is there, and to acknowledge is to have power.

To ignore the enemy is to invite him to have a foothold in your life, as Paul warns against. To allow anger to flow through your veins is to allow the devil to set a foundation in your heart. To be envious is to install a lens on your eyes through which you see material things and relationships in a way that builds a wall between you and God. Allowing sadness to grow and multiply creates hopelessness, ultimately leading to powerlessness and depression.

When nothing else in life makes sense, close your eyes and be at peace, knowing that the God of the Universe is there with you. He who created the stars and made the sun to shine its brilliant light will never leave you. Wake up each morning and acknowledge your tendencies, allowing the Holy Spirit to guide and help you overcome them. Yes, the sunrise is beautiful, but there is a spiritual war going on whether you recognize it consciously or not.

Make a daily effort to unwind the lies that the enemy has spun in your life. By doing that, you are stepping out of the dark and into your calling; you are, in effect, actively advancing the kingdom of God through your actions and efforts. What you are not doing, by contrast, is passively advancing the kingdom of our enemy.

Reflection Questions

- Do I allow God to be my gardener?
- Considering the fruits of the Spirit, where am I lacking?
- Do I remind myself daily that I was made for a specific purpose?

15

THE PATH OF PURITY

*Do not conform to the pattern of this world, but be transformed by
the renewing of your mind. Then you will be able to test and approve
what God's will is—his good, pleasing and perfect will.*

—Romans 12:2

My prayer is that, while reading this book, you will have
received validation that you have a role to play in pursuing
the kingdom of God. Your Heavenly Father knows that,
and so does your enemy. I pray that you will continue to
receive clarity regarding your gifts and how God would like
for you to use them in the advancement of His will for
mankind. I pray also that the unhealthy fruits of Satan's lies
have been made evident, so that you will see what must be
done to move into the freedom that comes with living according to your purpose.

The breath in your lungs is proof that God is not finished with you yet. So take the steps you must take in order
to grow and become more like Christ with each movement

and every thought. Start each day by asking God to renew your mind, so that you may test and approve what God's will is—His good, pleasing, and perfect will (Romans 12:2).

Psalm 119:9–16 provides us with a framework for entering into the presence of God and renewing our minds on a daily basis. In fact, it offers somewhat of a formula to help with consistency in our pursuit of God. We'll examine that Psalm verse by verse over the course of this chapter.

The truth is, whatever you do regularly becomes a part of who you believe yourself to be, whether that "something" is healthy or unhealthy. The tree you nourish most will become the strongest and the most difficult to chop down. Your life will ebb and flow with good and bad seasons, but the thing to remember through it all is that you are a garden; you were created for a purpose, and that truth comes with constantly choosing to better yourself for the sake of the kingdom of God. And unlike a garden in the literal sense, you, the created, have the opportunity to work alongside the Creator to grow and flourish. This growth happens along what is called the path of purity, which brings us to our study of King David's Psalm 119:9–16:

> How can a young person stay on the path of purity?
> (Psalm 119:9a)

The question that begins this passage draws the reader to a simple truth: if there is a right path to follow, it is the path of purity. But in a world filled with temptations, we know that it's just as simple to walk down other paths, most of which lead away from God.

So how does King David propose we remain true to the straight and narrow path? By living according to the Word of God (119:9b). What living means, literally, if we study the original Hebrew text, is that we are to guard the path of purity using the truth found in Scripture. Just as Paul later wrote in Ephesians, King David means that the Word of God is a sword meant for protecting the areas of life that connect us to God's heart and will. And before anything else, you and I must understand that our enemy is equipped with his weapons at all times.

The truths we must speak boldly are these and many more like them:

- I am the head, not the tail. (Deuteronomy 28:13)
- I am meant to be like a city on a hill. (Matthew 5:14)
- I have not received a spirit of fear, but the spirit of adoption. (Romans 8:15)

As we lean on the promises of God, it's our responsibility to be aware of the fact that we don't always notice the things causing us to backslide. We can offend others without realizing it, can't we? At times, it's not until we take a step back and reflect that we begin to see our tendencies to be impatient, stagnant, self-hating, isolated, hopeless, angry, envious, or ...?

The same can be said of sin. David knew this, which is why the next verse addresses what we can't see before approaching the things we can. It's as if he's suggesting that the less obvious, the hidden, the unintentional, is of primary importance when it comes to the renewal of our minds:

> I seek you with all my heart; do not let me stray from your commands. (Psalm 119:10)

This verse can be paraphrased as this: Lord, everything in me searches for you, but I'm human. I need you to help me to recognize the times I unknowingly sin against you.

Think about the word "stray." "Do not let me stray from your commands," David says. With this statement, he is intentionally seeking to get ahead of his natural tendency to wander. We do this today by inviting the Holy Spirit to convict us before our wandering can happen. This is a crucial step: submitting to His guidance and accepting the fact that we unknowingly sin each and every day.

So to remain on the path of purity, David is saying, "Yes, lean on the promises of God, but play your role as well." Like soldiers on a battlefield who have been given a directive by their general, we are still charged with being alert, smart with our strengths, and aware of our weaknesses—especially the ones that endanger us and those we love without our knowledge.

Next, King David speaks to intentional sin. These are the kinds we know exist and that already plague us, perhaps those things we don't work hard enough to rid ourselves of:

> I have hidden your words in my heart, that I might not sin against you. (Psalm 119:11)

When a choice was to be made—whether to commit an offense or to choose the path of purity—King David had already memorized God's truths and tucked them away in his heart for those times he knew he would need them the most. Sin that you acknowledge beforehand and choose to carry out is a conversation between you and God with you saying, "What I want is more important than what You want."

This is a narrative that Satan has written and he tries with every moment of life to subject you to it. Your flesh is weak and cannot be trusted, and that is the very reason why God's Word must be hidden like valuable treasure, engraved upon the surface of your heart for the moments when choices must be made—those which are contrary to what your flesh desires.

> Praise be to you, Lord; teach me your decrees. (Psalm 119:12)

This is such a beautiful verse, yet the true meaning can be missed due to the limitations of the English language.

The phrase, "Praise be to you," here is the same one we see in another familiar psalm where David says, "Bless the Lord, O my soul" (Psalm 103:1). It's literally a commandment of oneself to praise God.

In the original Hebrew, the word "bless" is a verb that can mean "kneel." This verse is drawing our attention to a posture we should assume when preparing for our minds to be renewed. This is not to say we should physically kneel every time we enter into the presence of God, though there would be nothing wrong with that; rather, this is a reminder that we should come to Him with our hearts in the posture of gratitude, giving honor and praise prior to receiving from Him.

> With my lips I recount all the laws that come from your mouth. (Psalm 119:13)

There is something powerful about praying and speaking the Word of God aloud. With your lips you ought to *declare* what God has revealed during the process of your mind being renewed. Everything He has spoken, whether new or old, is to be brought into the atmosphere by the voice given to you by God. There is a boldness in you that comes to life at the sound of your own voice taking ownership of what God has in store for you.

This practice is especially important when it comes to battling temptation and warring with the devil's kingdom. As you know, Satan's desire is the throne of God, and since he cannot have it, he will take every opportunity to use you as a tool to bring grief to the heart of God. By speaking the truth of your Father out loud, something incredible takes place and you begin to walk in an amount of courage you did not know you had.

The next verse speaks of cheerfulness. We have just seen that our process is to praise Him, then to boldly speak His promises, now the psalmist says that we ought to be cheerful in following the path of purity in the same way one is cheerful in wealth:

> I rejoice in following your statutes as one rejoices in great riches. (Psalm 119:14)

Riches ultimately bring a person joy because they provide a sense of security, but remember that the Lord is our ultimate source of confidence; riches pass away, but the path of purity leads to the fullness of life found in Christ.

The enemy will use earthly riches to distract us from receiving all that God has for us by introducing envy and covetousness into our lives. But we know, and ought to remind ourselves daily, that a life found in Christ is truly the only thing in the world worth envying. Make it a habit to choose joy and decide with each sunrise to find joy in obedience to God's commands.

The final two verses in this passage pertain to mindfulness, which appropriately conclude the ideas of this book:

I meditate on your precepts and consider your ways.
(Psalm 119:15)

Each and every day, in the process of your mind being renewed, make time to meditate on the things God has called you to, even if just for a few minutes, and never do so without afterwards considering the life of Jesus and the ways you can grow to be more like Him in your pursuit of the kingdom of God.

If you make this a conscious effort, if you decide each day to put to death the misdeeds of the body (Romans 8:13), then you will not play the passive role that the enemy would have you play in his kingdom.

I delight in your decrees; I will not neglect your word.
(Psalm 119:16)

Finally, do not ignore the Word of God. As mentioned in chapter six, "ignore" is what "neglect" means in this context. If God reveals something to you, something that requires change, don't just ignore it and push it out of your mind.

Take action.

Take ownership of your calling, your talents, your weaknesses, and address them with the amount of attention you know they each deserve. And remember: God has chosen us to advance His purpose for the world and it's our responsibility as the body of Christ to *uproot* the lies that suppress the greatness instilled in each of us. So let's go into battle together. Take up your sword and speak this truth over yourself today and every day:

I am good enough.

GRATITUDE

I have to begin by thanking my incredible wife, Stefanie. This book would not have been possible without her next to me, loving me, supporting my dreams, and encouraging me to live boldly.

My parents will always have my sincerest gratitude. I have nothing but the fondest memories of my childhood and would be far less than the man I am today without their commitment to raising me with such love and care. To my sister, Shelby: for always being there for me when I need you, no matter the distance between us.

I'm fortunate to have had two of the most outstanding, godly roommates in college, both of whom stood next to me as the "best man" in my wedding. This was either because I couldn't choose between them or because the three of us represent something unique and inseparable as a collective. Britton and Jonathon, I am eternally grateful for your friendship.

To Sam Stiles, I'm thankful for Chinese lunches, long work commutes, and obscure seasons. These were the things that allowed us to become such great friends. Our paths crossing was no accident and I look forward to many, many more years of being your brother in Christ. You're a good man to the core and an invaluable asset to the kingdom of God.

Many have contributed to my spiritual journey, but I would like to acknowledge four great men in particular. It's not about the fellowship or the wisdom they imparted to me, though those things are invaluable; it's about the manner in which they lived regardless of whether they knew I was watching. Thank you Pastor Josh Deeter, Blaine Lindsey, Jeff Rhodes, and Mark David Bradford.

To my editor, Nancy Pile, I am forever indebted not only to your editorial insight and expertise, but to your authentic heart and commitment to the message I hope to communicate. Whatever eternal impact this book is to have, you helped make it so.

Lastly, all my gratitude to the fictional men, women, and children who have allowed me to put the telling of their lives on hold while pursuing this book. With all I have learned through this process, I hope to capture your stories with a renewed eagerness and a heart full of wonder at everything you will achieve. Especially you, Samuel.

ABOUT THE AUTHOR

Nathan Madison lives in Birmingham, Alabama. He has a degree in international business from Auburn University and spent a summer in Beijing completing a minor in Chinese language. Nathan has explored careers in economic development and leisure travel but has not yet found another passion like writing. He loves dogs (especially those under five pounds), being in nature, and having meaningful late-night conversations with anyone willing to stay awake.

What was your experience reading this book? What helped you the most? If you would like to share, Nathan would love to hear from you at uprootbook@gmail.com.

Please also consider taking a few minutes to post a review of Uproot on Amazon. Your feedback and support will help Nathan to improve his writing craft for future books.

CPSIA information can be obtained
at www.ICGtesting.com
Printed in the USA
LVHW042109200421
685051LV00002B/5